elevate

a simple meditation to increase happiness and abundance in your life

Copyright © 2017 by Nina Englander. All Rights Reserved.
No part of this publication may be reproduced, distributed, or transmitted in any form or by any means, including photocopying, recording, or other electronic or mechanical methods, or by any information storage and retrieval system without the prior written permission of the publisher, except in the case of very brief quotations embodied in critical reviews and certain other noncommercial uses permitted by copyright law.

Cover illustration © Samantha Wilder Oliver

ISBN 978-0-9991056-0-3

What's Inside

For Ronna.

PROLOGUE
Elevate

ELEVATE.

Science has demonstrated again and again that the practice of meditation is beneficial to our health and well-being. Meditation reduces stress, increases happiness, and has been shown to improve cardiovascular and immune health. That's just to name a few of its attributes. However, even with the increased popularity of meditation in the mainstream, many people think they "can't" meditate. They feel it's too difficult, takes up too much time (that they don't have), or requires a highly attentive brain (which they also don't have). If this is you, I feel your pain.

Welcome to Elevate! Elevate is a simple, quick meditation that combines mental images with physical sensations. Elevate is easy to learn, easy to do, and can serve as a quick reset for your mind as you go through your day. Elevate can be done in less than five minutes, and can be a sustainable practice for even the busiest and most distracted among us.

Elevate uses a visualization exercise that runs through your seven chakras – or energy centers in your body – from the base of your spine to the top of your head. It's kind of like an upside-down "roto-rooter" of the spirit. It enables you to get all the icky stuff out and in turn fill yourself back up with everything good.

Practiced daily, Elevate will slow-drip positive thoughts into your subconscious and will ultimately move you towards more happiness in your life. The best thing about Elevate is that it only takes a few minutes each day to practice, so it is sustainable even for busy people!

The Elevate process is a highly edited form of meditation. Do not confuse Elevate with a traditional meditation practice – it is something quite different. Of course, it can take years, even decades, to develop a successful and meaningful meditation practice. Elevate is more of an anchor--a quick reminder to be in the present moment, a quick clarifier of goals and dreams, and a quick way to raise your emotional vibration. Most importantly, it is a mood elevator. It is time-efficient and easy to learn. And, if you desire, you can use it as a stepping stone into the world of mindfulness meditation.

This book is not a how-to on mindfulness meditation. It is not a theoretical book of quantum physics or education or philosophy. Rather, Elevate is a workbook that will teach you a new method for bringing more peace and happiness into each and every day. The bulk of this book includes the preparation to Elevate. As with many practices in life, preparing to Elevate takes a little bit of time, but once you have some planning behind you, the process is easy.

Elevate will take you on a journey. Take this opportunity to slow down for a few moments and think about your life, your goals and dreams, and the things that make you smile on the inside – and then join me in making the daily commitment to Elevate!

PART 1
Why We Elevate

GOING DOWN THE STRESS RABBIT HOLE AND LEARNING HOW TO COME BACK OUT.

One night, I was feeling stressed about money and couldn't sleep. I can't stand stressing about money. The only thing I dislike more than stressing about money is stressing about the thought of having no money.

Here I was, trying to get to sleep – a time to relax, have happy thoughts, and drift off towards a peaceful eight hours – and all I could think about was managing my current financial situation. I had certain bills due all at once, two teenagers asking for this and that, credit card debt, and on top of everything I was running my own business – need I say more? Oh yeah, and taxes.

I know you understand what I am saying. We all understand this stress – whether we have a lot or a little, financial stress is part of our human experience. But this kind of stress is not helpful or productive for us in any way.

The physical response to stress almost always comes not from the actual situation, but instead from the perception of the situation. Stress comes from the story that our brain tells us about what is happening. And stress can be destructive on both the thoughts and the body.

As a chiropractor, I see first-hand what stress does to people. I witness a lot of people who are in pain or feeling imbalanced and are struggling to heal in some way. Over the last twenty-five years, I have learned again and again that there are many different reasons why physical problems arise. A person is as likely to be "thrown off" by an argument with a family member as he is to be "thrown off" by a car accident, although one may seem more obviously damaging than the other. The physical pain may be real, and the source of the pain may be real, but the underlying cause of that pain can often occur from one's emotions.

When I first got my degree, I was working as a health consultant for a nutritional supplement company. One morning, out of the blue, I woke up with severe knee pain in both legs. I had never experienced anything like it before. It was difficult and painful to walk, and I was struggling to manage the pain. I was unable to go to work for a week. I sought out different practitioners to help me find out the source of this pain. I tried chiropractic, acupuncture, and massage, but still I got no relief. I even had X-rays taken; all was normal. I saw my medical doctor and was told I had a "virus" in my knees, something I never knew was possible. Finally I went to a homeopath. He sat down with me, looked me in the eye, and asked, "So, what's going on in your life?" I burst out crying – in my long quest for healing, no one had asked me that question. What was going on in my life? Well, I was living with my boyfriend, who was out of work (he was an artist and needed the day-job-to-make-money-for-rent kind of work). I had agreed to carry the expenses of our household while he looked for a job. The job-search was taking much longer than he had anticipated, and I was holding up more and more of the responsibility of the household finances for the two of us. When I peeled away the "Oh, it's fine, I don't mind" layer and got down to how I really felt, the truth was that I felt put upon and taxed financially. Ultimately, I felt that he was taking advantage of me. For many reasons, I didn't feel comfortable expressing any of that to him. The homeopath let me talk and cry for over an hour. When I was done, he replied, "Do you still think you have a virus in your knees?"

He gave me a homeopathic remedy, which I took diligently, and yet nothing changed. I was still in pain and pretty bummed out about it. However, I was much more aware of the emotional conflict in my life, my inability to speak up for myself, and my complicated feelings about money, which were coming right up to me and knocking on my head. I started seeing a therapist and working through some of these important issues. And, this is the honest truth: the day my boyfriend got a new job, my knee pain vanished. Literally, as quickly as it came on, it was gone.

That experience taught me more about healing than four years of graduate school. True healing necessitates looking at the body as not just a body but as both body and mind as a unit. Emotions, family, relationships, and work all affect our health. But money issues take the cake. Stressing about money – not having enough of it, fighting with loved ones about it, paying out large amounts of it for health insurance, college, or taxes – all of these issues – make people sick. People with financial stress (significant or not) can have lower back pain, menstrual irregularities, trouble with the lower digestive system, and problems with their legs, knees, or feet. Stress around finances has become a chronic illness, and the prevalence of this chronic illness is making our society sick. If we had healthier feelings about money, we would be a healthier society.

Every day, I spend a lot of time dishing out advice and tips for how people can deal better with their stressful feelings. I talk about how to reframe situations or how to channel energy into a more positive direction. So that night while I was lying in bed and spiraling down the rabbit hole, I thought, "Englander, get it together. Practice what you preach!" Why couldn't I do it myself? What came to me at that moment was the idea for a quick and easy meditation – a re-alignment of my thoughts – to divert negative, stressful feelings into more positive ones. I knew instantly that this could be a tool for relieving stress in the moment and could also be used for growth and expansion for my patients, my friends, and most immediately, for me.

I started with a simple mental exercise – a basic visualization meditation. (It always has to be simple with me, or I won't do it.) I worked my way up from the base of my spine, focusing on the energy centers in my body and thinking of images that made me happy. In minutes, using this new tool, I felt redirected and centered. I had a sense of ease and – most importantly – I felt happier. I slipped into a peaceful sleep with a smile on my face.

The next day was my wedding anniversary, and my husband and I went out for a nice dinner to celebrate. It was an exceptionally tasty meal. In our celebratory state, and feeling generous with our good vibes, we sent a note to the chef thanking him for such a delicious and wonderful experience. (I had never done that before!) The chef was so grateful that he gave us oysters and dessert on the house.

Here is my favorite money metaphor: When you take a shower, do you know where every drop of water is coming from? Unless you are a civil engineer, probably not. But just because you don't know how the water is coming, it doesn't stop you from planning to take your daily shower and trusting that the water will come out of the showerhead.

My first thought was, "Wow, that was quick. The universe is already sending more abundance my way, and it hasn't even been twenty-four hours!" It wasn't a check or a wad of cash, but it didn't have to be. Because of my meditation the night before, I was more open to noticing that sweet cosmic wink.

The following week, I was working with a patient who was stressed because she and her husband were feeling a big financial pinch. Her language reflected how high-strung she was about the situation. "We are scraping the bottom of the barrel here," she said to me one day. I suggested my meditation to her; I asked her to try taking all that negative energy around her lack of money and channeling it into more positive feelings. I had her visualize having more money without worrying about how she was going to obtain it. I also had her think about what it would feel like once she had more money. She came up with a picture in her head. Then I had her concentrate on how it felt in her body when she looked at that picture of ease, happiness, and abundance.

About an hour later, she called to tell me that while she was in my office, her husband had gotten a statement in the mail from a company in which they had made a small investment decades ago. They had totally forgotten about it. The statement showed they had earned $7,000.00!

I am using money as the main metaphor here, but there is more to the magic of life besides finding/attracting/earning/discovering money. Money allows us to easily quantify the magic, but magic can be found anywhere as long as we are tuned in to see it. Athletes often use the concept of imagery as a way to meet their physical and mental goals. They focus their minds on the goal whether it's crossing the finish line, making a ball go through a basket, or completing a downhill ski run. Athletes perform these skills in their minds often enough that their bodies believe they experience the outcome. The results can be amazing. The process has worked so well (and gotten so popular) that in the 2014 Winter Olympic Games the US brought nine sports psychologists to Sochi to assist the ninety-three athletes in the imagery process.* Some Olympians even used mental imagery after injuries to help them heal.

So, while chiropractic is a very effective form of natural health care, and aligning the spine is good for the body's structure and function, physical alignment is not the only practice necessary for good health and happiness. Our emotional alignment affects our circumstances, as well as our health, sometimes in very profound ways. This is the idea behind Elevate. Elevate is a tool for emotional alignment. Elevate gives you a process to follow, a template with which to make it successful, and an opening of your awareness for why, when, and how often magic shows up in your life.

**NYT 2/22/14 Olympians Use Imagery as Mental Training. By Christopher Clarey.*

HOW WE THINK.

Elevate requires that we spend a few minutes each day thinking a little differently.

Everyone thinks. But how do we think? We understand that we think with our brains. The brain is an organ that weighs about three pounds and resides inside your skull. The brain is a brilliant piece of machinery, controlling all of the processes in the body and running an electrical network so vast that we only understand a tiny fraction of what it does. Twenty-four hours a day and seven days a week, the brain runs the central nervous system, all of the muscles, organs, glands, and blood vessels. But what is it that does the thinking?

When we think, we are actually using the mind. The mind is harder to understand than the brain. The mind is not so much a thing, but more of an action. Some of what the mind does occurs in the brain and some occurs elsewhere in the body. The mind encompasses the conscious, the subconscious, and the connection between both with the physical body. The body is thereby considered part of the mind.

Conscious Mind

Our conscious mind includes the senses – the way we get information from the outside world. They are, of course, sight, sound, touch, smell, taste and movement. If we were to live merely through these six senses, we would be living a life based on instinct and survival, no different from the rest of the animal kingdom. What separates us is our intellectual faculties: Our abilities to reason, perceive, imagine, remember, create discipline and focus, and have intuition. Much like our muscles, these six faculties are developed over time, and with use and practice, they grow and get stronger. It is these intellectual faculties that allow us to be higher-level thinkers. And just like our muscles, if we don't use them, they shrink.

Subconscious Mind and Physical Body.
Our subconscious mind is our non-thinking mind or our feeling mind. The subconscious mind is where all of our belief systems reside. This is where we store our paradigms – belief systems that have become habits. We operate largely from our subconscious paradigms. However, those subconscious paradigms originate from our thoughts.

In other words, it is our thoughts that influence feelings. Feelings cause discrete chemical reactions in the physical body as certain areas of the brain are triggered to dump various neurotransmitters and hormones into the bloodstream. The body, in turn, responds to those chemical changes with alterations in heart rate, blood pressure, stomach acid secretion – as well as thousands of other changes that are currently unknown – thus creating change in the body's vibration.

How thoughts become things.
Vibration in the body can ultimately change our actions. Taking different actions sets us up for different results.

When our emotions signal frustration, fear, sadness, anger, or another negative emotion, it causes a negative vibration in our body. The actions we take from that perspective, or vibration, will be very different than the actions we might take when our emotions signal excitement, inspiration, joy and possibility. As you will read later, the vibration we give off can also affect who and what we attract into our life.

Crusty, funky, money talk.
Once again, money is the easiest metaphor with which to describe the subconscious mind and the paradigms it deeply holds. I possess some intense, crusty, funky beliefs around money. I was raised by a single mom who worked very hard to support us. She did her best and yet I was raised with the message that we were poor and did not have enough. My deeply-held paradigm includes the fact that money is finite; if you spend too much of it, it will run out. So don't spend it!

Not long ago, my husband and I went to lease a new car and, throughout the transaction, while we were signing papers and making choices about interior and exterior colors, he kept asking me if I was angry at him. He asked me, "Is it that you don't want this kind of car? Are you feeling OK? Are you mad at me?" I took a deep breath and realized that my whole body language had become sullen and smoldering and uncomfortable. This was the energy I was giving off as a result of being face-to-face with a large expenditure of money. (Even though we were just replacing one expiring lease with another!) I tried to envision my infinite shower of money-water, put a smile on my face, and apologized on behalf of my crusty paradigm. There is always work left to be done!

Harnessing the power of thinking.

Ultimately, we choose the thoughts we consciously think. Our thoughts, then, unconsciously influence our feelings. Our feelings influence our actions, and our actions create our results. Are you as happy as you want to be? Are you as successful, as loved, as strong and fit, as well-read?

Many people think that in order to get different results you just need to take different actions. But the truth is that you will not consistently take different actions unless you change your belief systems and the ingrained emotions residing in your subconscious mind. Realigning these beliefs is not an easy task, as you probably know if you are human. To begin making a big change, you need to start thinking different thoughts.

> **Thoughts become Things.** *You become what you think about the most. No one ever taught you how to think when you were a kid. How would your life be different if someone had?*

Our mind thinks in pictures.

Most people think in pictures. There is a huge plasma TV screen in the window of your mind. If I tell you to think of a banana, you picture a banana. If I tell you to think of a pine tree, you picture a pine tree. If we are trying to change our beliefs, paradigms, and emotions, we need to start by choosing the pictures we want to be watching on our internal TV.

Conjuring a mental image may come more easily to some people than others, but like the intellectual faculty of imagination, it is a muscle that can be exercised and improved with practice.

Try this exercise: *Picture in your mind a person who you deeply love. Sit with that picture for a moment. How does this feel in your body? Do you feel a shift in vibration? Can you feel your heart tingle a little? Now imagine where you were when the Twin Towers came down on 9/11 (or if you are too young to remember, picture the video clips you have seen on TV.) Did you feel a shift? It is instantaneous. It is neurological. It is physiological. (Please go back to a happy image before reading on to reset your physiology to a more positive vibration.)*

Creating a mental image is like having a shortcut on your desktop. With a shortcut, you can click once on an application to open it, instead of having to navigate through the hard drive to find it. Since mental imagery has the power to immediately change your physiology, you can use the shortcut to your advantage to help quickly change your vibration. Elevate is the shortcut for meditation. It is a quick shot of mindfulness, combined with images that you project on your inner plasma screen TV. Isn't it amazing that you have all this high-tech equipment conveniently located in your brain?

Fake it 'Til you Make it.

In the beginning of chiropractic training, students have to learn how to feel the different parts of the spine. This is a difficult new task for most people. All the science and philosophy is one thing, but actually putting your hands on another human being and hunting around in the topography of their bones is a whole other ball of wax. Very early on, one of my teachers suggested that if I couldn't get the feel for it I should simply act "as if" I could feel it. She said that eventually, if I faked it enough, it would start to come to me naturally. I was only twenty-three when I first got that wise advice, and I have found it helpful again and again in my skills and in my life. Using repetition and positive thinking, I created a pattern in my mind for understanding what the spine felt like. Elevate uses the same concept. By using pictures consistently, even if they are "fakes" at first, you will create a new pattern (and a new paradigm) in your mind that will start to come naturally.

Like any skill, even the easiest of processes takes a little while to master. When you begin to Elevate, be patient. If you can't feel your vibration at first, act "as if" you can. I promise that, little by little, it will soon become second nature to you.

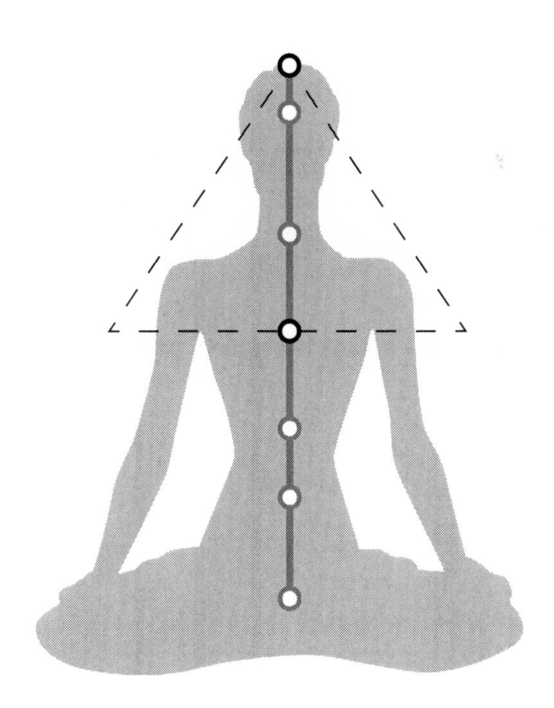

PREPARING FOR THE PROCESS.

1. **Creating your roadmap.**

   The first thing you need in order to get from where you are to where you want to be is a map. As you begin your elevate adventure, you will first need to take some time to create your map. No one's map is the same as anyone else's. Also, your own map today may look different from your map next Thursday. But regardless, you will need a map to begin your journey.

   The first part of creating your map involves reading this book. In Part II of the book, I explain in detail how to create your roadmap by using visual images, emotions, and energy. In each chapter I have given you the tools to manufacture your own perfect roadmap. At the end of each section, there is a list of possible questions for you to answer as a way to generate ideas. You can answer any of the questions that resonate with you. Answer in your head or out loud to a partner. Better yet, write down your answers. Get as creative as you wish, whether it's with words or art or some other medium. I have also provided some suggestions that may help you come up with visual ideas for Elevate images. I offer some tools, but know that only you can create your perfect mental pictures (and your emotional connection to those pictures).

2. **Make the time for it.**

   Bad news first. In order to develop a good and sustainable Elevate roadmap, you will need to devote up to an hour or two. Take some time to read these chapters and use the workbook questions and suggestions. Block off an hour in your schedule. Create an event in Google Calendar and invite yourself. Or you can make a play-date with a friend and do it together. Make the time for it, and the process will pay off. You will only need to do this once (until you are ready to change your goals, desires and dreams).

The good news is that once you have prepared you can Elevate in just a few minutes. You can do it when you are sitting on a train, relaxing in the parking lot before work, or at your child's dance recital or baseball game (don't tell them, of course, that you are not paying rapt attention to them). It's like a woman exercising her pelvic floor muscles: no one needs to know she's doing it, but it is always extremely helpful! You can Elevate at a certain time each day, like when you are in the shower or brushing your teeth. Or you can do it in a special place, like hiking in the woods with your dog or sitting in your garden. You can even make this process a ritual to do while you are getting ready to drift off to sleep at night.

If you feel like your life is too busy to do this step (is that how far off-track we have gotten that we cannot find one to two hours for ourselves?) just make a commitment to yourself that you will spend one to two fewer hours on Facebook or Candy Crush or Zappos this week. It is amazing how much time gets sucked out of our lives by technology and how much time we find when we take a technology break.

Once you understand the process in your head, you will be able to fly through it and activate all of your energy centers one by one (using visual images and emotional connections) in just a matter of minutes. If you do it once a day (or more), you will start to see elements in your life begin to change – sometimes in ways you have never even imagined.

❸ Is it a meditation?

This process is a meditation. Once again, it is not to be confused with a traditional mindfulness meditation practice. Elevate is designed to get you into a focused and mindful state for a few minutes. Elevate will briefly take your mind out of the rat race and into a place where you can imagine and feel incredibly positive thoughts and images. Elevate is a short vacation for the mind intended to shift your vibration to one of greater positivity, hopefulness, and love.

❹ Alignment.

OK, yes, I am a chiropractor, so it's all about alignment for me. And that is why this is a perfect segue for me to go from aligning the spine and nervous system to Elevate – aligning the spirit, goals, and dreams. The more aligned your images are with each other, the more you can focus your intention, and hence, the more magic will happen. If your intention is to be healthier, your images can align around how you will feel when you have more energy and more vitality. If your goal is to have more success, your images can align around a project you want to complete or a person you admire. If your hope is to be happier, your images can reflect elements or people in your life that bring you joy.

❺ Magic.

The amazing thing about this process is that you don't have to wait until you are finished creating the roadmap for magic to start happening. Magical events will start happening in your life the second you decide to start this process. Actually, magical things happen constantly in our lives. It's just that most of the time we are too busy or distracted to notice them. When you use your intention, making this alignment part of your day will bring you into a vibration that allows you to better notice everyday miracles and magic.

❻ Enjoy it!

Doing the Elevate meditation feels good – that is largely the point. The act should also be enjoyable. The Elevate process wants to bring a smile to your face. If it becomes a chore, the process is out of alignment and needs to be altered (kind of like life). In fact, the process is meant to be adjusted so it can flow with your changing goals, desires and dreams.

GOALS, DESIRES AND DREAMS.

Elevate will help you manifest your goals, desires, and dreams, whether they are tangible (like having more money, a loving partner, or more defined butt muscles) or emotional (like feeling better about yourself, letting go of anger, or bringing peace to an unhappy relationship). The bottom line is that Elevate leads to a higher vibration, which ultimately brings more goodness into your life.

The high vibration of happiness.

If your goal is to be happier, you will want to choose images that raise your vibration and make you feel the feeling of happiness.

> *You might choose an image of adorable children embracing you, your dog wagging her tail at you ecstatically, or a special place that makes you feel warm and fuzzy inside. The key is to see the image in your mind and feel the wonderful emotion it evokes.*

An image is just a mirage. But the feeling that an image evokes is real. The good news is that your subconscious mind does not know the difference between a feeling that is based on a tangible element and a feeling that is based on an image that only exists in your mind's eye. It's the same feeling either way.

If you are trying to manifest more money in your life, it is adequate to visualize a bank statement and the high balance in your account. Better yet, picture a particular aspect of life that money will provide, like a new home or something you've always wanted but felt you couldn't afford, like a new pair of expensive shoes (if you're me) or a vacation to an exotic land (if you're my husband). Or you can conjure an image of a large donation (picturing the actual check or money order) that you will make from your lofty bank account to a charity that you want to support.

Instead of just picturing the statement, the new home, or the donation check, try to feel the emotion that the image brings you. That is the trick.

Feel the sense of accomplishment in watching your bank account grow. See yourself in your new home and feel the enjoyment of it. Imagine looking fantastic in your new shoes (or trying not to trip in them). Imagine yourself on a sandy beach looking for rare sea animals or trekking up a mountain in Nepal. Imagine what it will feel like to know that you have just given generously to someone in need.

It takes imagination and focus, which is ultimately what will help you Elevate. You can change the images to match what you truly want to bring about in your life. The most important thing is to find the feeling you are trying to create in your life, and then feel it.

Chakras and the importance of balancing energy.

With Elevate, you will create emotional imagery and run it through the chakra system – 7 energy centers in your body. Running pictures through each of the seven chakras provides a structure for your meditation, and offers a daily energy clearing of your entire body. It is like dental floss for your spirit. We will discuss the chakras in more detail in a later chapter.

GUIDELINES FOR GOAL-SETTING AND IMAGE-CREATING.

1. **Be authentic when defining your goals.**

The goals you set – no matter how well-meaning and appropriate they may seem – are worthless if they are not authentic to you. When you Elevate, only create visual images that feel real to you.

Let's say your mother always wanted you to be a doctor (not uncommon in my tribe of origin). You, in your heart of hearts, don't really want to be a doctor and know that you get dizzy at the sight of blood. But you love and respect your mother (as you should) so you go ahead and create a visual image of yourself in an operating room with scrubs on preparing to cut into someone's abdomen. If you don't truly want the outcome, your brain will go completely out of alignment and set up a negative vibration around this image. "I am a doctor" may be the image you are bringing up, but "I hate the sight of blood" is still sitting in your subconscious mind. Your mind declares war, and the subconscious wins. The subconscious mind always wins, by the way.

This is different from the "fake it 'til you make it" concept. Slow-dripping an image of something you really want – even though it hasn't happened yet – will help you change your behavior and your circumstances. Slow-dripping an image of something that someone else wants for you probably will not.

2. **What is "possible"?**

Something is only possible if you believe that it is possible. In my healing practice, I know that what every person needs from me on their first visit is hope. That person needs to know that, no matter what diagnosis she has been given by her physician, Dr. Oz, or WebMD, that there is a possibility that she can get better, feel better, be happier, and have a better life.

When we think about the life we want to create and what it takes to get there, we have a funny balancing act to do. On one hand, we want to look at the possibilities; is there a possibility that you could become a professional dancer, a millionaire, a Nobel Prize recipient? That answer has to be "yes" before you can align around it. If you think it is possible, it is. That doesn't mean it's necessarily going to happen. But it is possible that it can happen – and only if it is possible will it happen.

On the other hand, we don't want to cross things off of our list of desires just because they may seem impossible at first. As Dr. Srini Pillay explains, "if the pot of gold is located on the other side of the mountain, sometimes we have to start climbing the mountain before we can see, from our new vantage point, that it is possible to get to the pot of gold." In other words, sometimes things that don't seem possible in the moment will seem more possible the closer we get to them.

3 Be sensible.

When preparing to Elevate, you don't want to set your first goal so high that it is not attainable. Then you run the risk of setting up a negative cycle that becomes essentially, "I used to have that goal, but it wasn't attainable so screw it, I'm done. I'll never be a dancer, a poet laureate, President." I call that the Eeyore affect; "Oh, bother." You want to write the next 'Hamilton" and have it open on Broadway? Start by setting a smaller goal, like writing for community theater. If you really want to be President of the United States (and it's not just your mother's big idea), you can start by setting a smaller goal, like running for local government. This goal, although it has less star-power, is a clear stepping-stone toward the greater goal.

4. **Take action.**

Of course, you cannot reach your goals with visualization and positive outlook alone. You have to engage, act, and take risks to see your goals realized. Often you have to fail before you reach your goals. But doing the work of visualizing, dreaming, journaling, creating, believing – the work of mindful preparation – will set up the right vibration for opportunities, helpful people, fantastic ideas, and unexpected resources to come your way. Quickly and easily. This is the magic of Elevate and the magic of life.

WHAT'S THE PROCEDURE HERE?

At my wedding reception, my ninety-four year-old grandfather stood before a crowd of 150 people, knife held high over a giant challah, and inquired in his thick Yiddish accent, "Now, vat's the procedure here?"

This is the question, especially if you've never meditated before. There is a procedure in learning to Elevate. And as with learning other processes, there will be a learning curve. Certain things are easy to learn, but everything takes time to master.

First Steps to Elevate. *First, you'll want to practice playing with energy in your body. Find a quiet time and a quiet space. Sit comfortably with your hands on your thighs. Make sure you are not so comfortable that you risk falling asleep! Take a few good breaths. A good breath goes into the belly first (not the chest). Fill up the lower and middle (side) lungs first and then the chest. Feel the oxygen going where it needs to go.*

Now for the energy. Bring your awareness to your hands resting on your thighs. See if you can generate heat in your palms against your thighs just by thinking about it. With intention, you can bring energy to any area. It may feel weak or funny at first, but like anything, this process takes practice. Alternatively, you may find that you are a natural at creating energy, and it's a piece of cake for you.

Feel the energy or heat in your hands and bring your hands together, or rub them quickly together (think Scouts trying to light a fire with two sticks.) See if you can feel a "buzzing" or vibrating sensation between your hands. Once you feel the energy between your hands, start spreading them apart and see if you can feel a ball of energy that gets bigger as you separate your hands wider.

Now, take your buzzing hands and place them on your belly, up near your ribs. Try to feel the ball of energy buzz into your stomach. This is the energy we are going to use to Elevate. Learn what it feels like. Practice making it come and go in different places in your body.

Focusing the mind.
The other piece of Elevate that will need some practice is focusing your mind. As with other more traditional meditations, the object is not to stop your mind from wandering. Your mind will wander; that's what the mind naturally does. The practice of mindfulness meditation means learning how to re-focus and re-direct the wandering mind back to the moment at hand. Be aware of the mind going off on tangents and then continue the practice of going back to the present moment.

It is good to have an anchor, something that reminds you to be mindful. In other types of meditation, the breath can be the anchor, or a mantra (a word or phrase repeated over and over), or counting to ten and back down to one, again and again. Each time the focus drifts, go back to the breath. Or the mantra. Or the counting. Sharon Salzberg, well-known teacher and writer in the world of meditation, says when you have to do that again and again, that is your practice.

In Elevate, we use mental pictures, along with the seven chakras, as our anchors. Having several elements stimulating us at once can be a little daunting at first, but remember that practice is necessary in order to become a master. If you find your mind getting distracted, which it will, go back to the chakras and pictures.

Feeling energy at the same time as visualizing something can be a challenge for some people. First, try experiencing them one at a time, then alternate the pictures and vibration. Ultimately, you will be able to experience them both and the emotions that go with them. This is the turbo-charge of Elevate – a combined stimulus with power to shift you further than you thought you could go!

Using this book.
You can use the workbook pages throughout this book to create a personal set of mental images with which to anchor your meditation. You will learn about the chakras, where each one is located, and what each one symbolizes in your life. You will spend some time visioning goals, the future you want, the emotions you would like to feel, and what it would mean for you to be happier (more fulfilled, more abundant, more loved, etc.).

When you put it all together on your "cheat sheet," **Elevate will look like this**:

Sit down and find your bearings.
Start to breathe.
Generate some energy. Start in your hands and then bring it into your body.
Elevate. Starting from Chakra 1, working up to Chakra 7 - Feel the buzz in each chakra and visualize the image for that chakra.
End with a moment of Gratitude/Appreciation.

Once you have fine-tuned your personal Elevate process, it can take only a few minutes to do the whole practice. Of course, you can take as much time as you'd like. Elevate feels good, changes the brain's biochemistry, and functions as a much-needed time-out for busy people. Chances are you will want more than a few minutes, but it can be done very quickly and easily. At least for me, something that is quick and easy is much more likely to become a habit!

Enjoy Elevate so you can enjoy more of life.

PART 2
How to Elevate

CHAKRAS

In Sanskrit, the word chakra means "wheel." The chakras in your body are wheels of energy. There are seven main chakras, which align with the spine, starting from the tailbone and going up to the top of the head. To visualize a chakra in the body, imagine a small, swirling funnel of energy, like a happy, gentle tornado of life-force.

You can change how the energy moves in a chakra by tuning in to it. If you focus your concentration on a certain energy center, you can actually "awaken" it, making it buzz, hum, or vibrate. Elevate gives you exercises that open each chakra by focusing the mind and finding the buzz. Stimulating the seven chakras will lead to an increased feeling of well-being and is an excellent daily health practice mentally, physically, and spiritually.

Each of the seven chakras corresponds with an area of the spine. However, chakras – which are three-dimensional – also include bundles of nerves and major organs and are integral to our physical health. Chakras relate to our psychological, emotional, and spiritual states of being, as well. It is essential that our chakras stay open and aligned. If there is a blockage, energy does not flow, and backup and stagnation will occur.

In her book *Anatomy of the Spirit*, Carolyn Myss details how imbalances in each chakra can relate to specific physical problems in the body. She likens the chakra system to an electrical switchboard. Imagine that for each energy center in your body, you have a certain number of plugs, each going to a different organ or body region. For the first chakra, for instance, you have one plug that goes to your colon, one that goes to your bladder, and one that goes to your legs. When your energy is blocked, it's as if one of those plugs has come out of the switchboard. This blockage can lead to problems like constipation, chronic bladder infections, or sciatica. Understanding why a chakra (like a drain) can get blocked or clogged, can be a key to healing that area of the body. If you can clear that energy, it's like sticking the plug back in and starting to heal again.

There are many practices that use visualization and imagery as a tool for meditation, goal-setting, and healing. I find that combining visualization with tuning into the chakra system creates a beautiful structure – already built in – that makes Elevate highly effective. Elevate is easy to learn and easy to do, therefore it is easy to sustain as a regular daily practice.

What makes a chakra meditation effective is focusing the energy in that chakra or "activating" the energy center. To understand what activated energy feels like, try the exercise of quickly rubbing your hands together. When you start generating some heat between your hands, move them a few inches apart and see if you can feel the energy between them. I call that the "hum" or the "buzz." Make a ball of energy between your hands and move it around; make it wider and thinner, or move it to the right and left. Now take that ball of energy and hold it over your belly, pushing it into your body. See if you can feel the hum or buzz in your belly. Once you complete this movement a couple of times, you will be able to start the hum just with your mind by focusing your attention on the area. It takes practice.

If you have trouble finding the vibration, try visualizing light or warmth going to the chakra. The result is the same. The key is the focus.

When you Elevate, you will be creating a "hum" in each of the seven chakras while visualizing positive images that relate to that chakra. Think of this exercise as turbo-charging your vibration and taking your vibration to the next level!

Here are the chakras and where you can find them on your body:

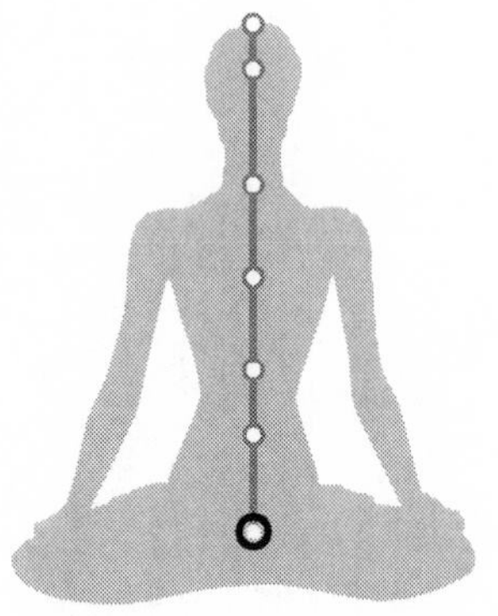

FIRST CHAKRA.

The first chakra, or the root chakra, is located down where your tail would be if you had one. If you sit on the ground, your root chakra is the energetic part of you that feels as if you could put down virtual roots into the earth. It is an energy center at the base of your coccyx and includes the pelvic floor. I am trying to avoid it, but I just have to say it: it is around your "bum."

The first chakra represents our connection to our tribe, our ancestors both living and not living, and our sense of safety and stability in life. It also represents our connection to material things.

The first chakra hum: *Bring your attention down into the area of the first chakra and getting the vibration going. Really feel it-you might feel the sensation of buzzing or vibration down at the bottom of your tailbone or in the perineal area. Or, as I like to say, bring the hum into your bum!*

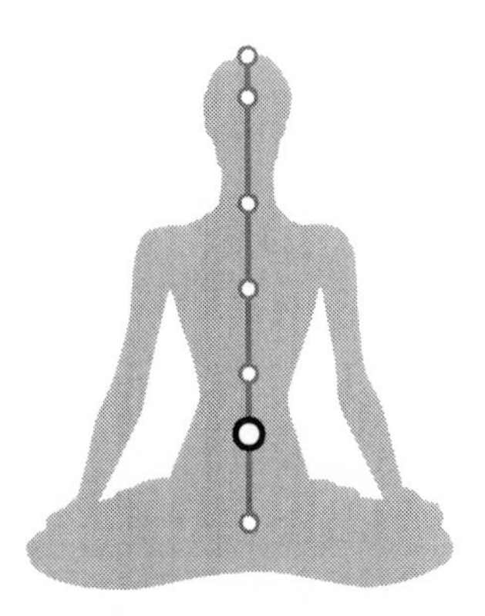

SECOND CHAKRA.

The second chakra is located in the lower abdomen and lower back. Because we are talking about energy that goes through structures like radio waves, the front and back of the body are irrelevant. The second chakra also has influence over the male and female reproductive organs.

The second chakra represents creativity, fertility, and emotion. It is also considered the chakra of power, sex, and money, especially the emotional aspect of money.

The second chakra hum: *Bring the hum into the pelvic area deep into the abdomen between your navel and pubic bone, around the area where the uterus resides, or would reside if you are a person who doesn't have one.*

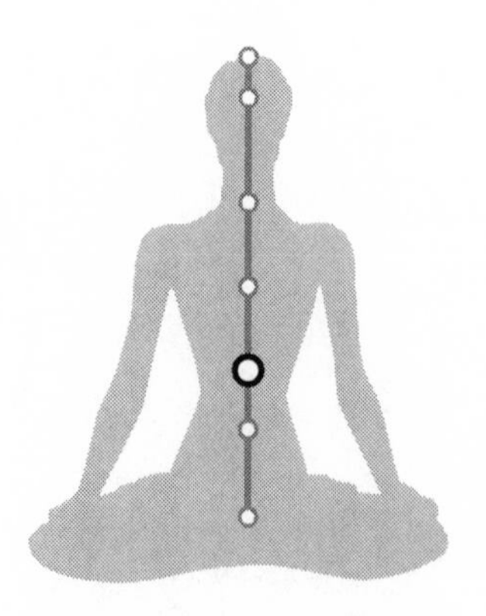

THIRD CHAKRA.

The third chakra is located in the belly and around the back lower ribs and diaphragm. This chakra is located in the solar plexus, known as the center of the body. It is also known in Chinese medicine as the DanTian.

The third chakra represents the ego or the self. This is the source of power, self-esteem, and self-worth.

The third chakra hum: *This is the energetic area in your belly, which you can find in the center of your body. You can feel the hum at the top of the stomach, just under the diaphragm.*

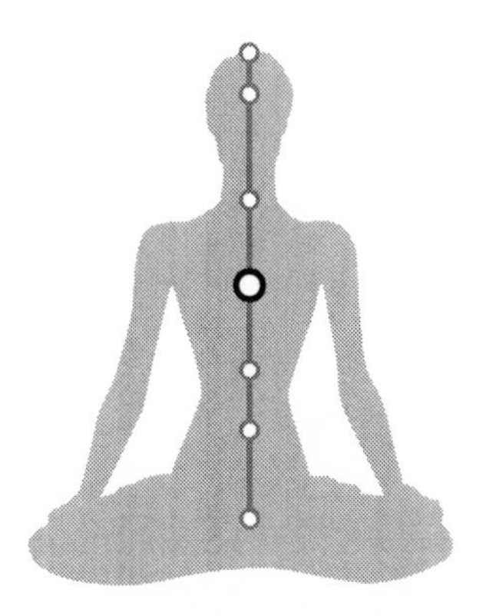

FOURTH CHAKRA.

The fourth chakra is located in the heart center.

The fourth chakra represents love, giving, and forgiveness.

The fourth chakra hum: *The hum is in the center of the chest. Even though the literal heart is way over to the left, the energetic heart is right in the middle. This is a very easy buzz to get for most people. You can accentuate it by thinking of someone you love deeply (or someone who loves you) at the same time as you gather the energy there.*

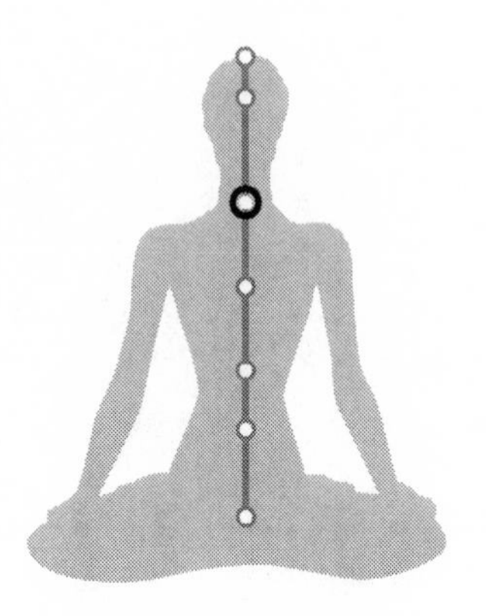

FIFTH CHAKRA.

The fifth chakra is located in the throat, from below the chin, down around the thyroid gland, and down the neck, including vocal chords, glands and the neck vertebrae and muscles.

The fifth chakra represents the ability to communicate and the expression of will.

The fifth chakra hum: *The hum is in the center of the throat.*

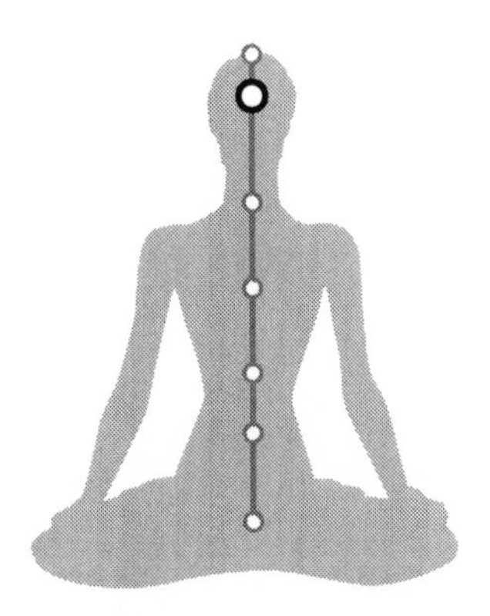

SIXTH CHAKRA.

The sixth chakra is located between your eyebrows at your "third eye." The sixth chakra includes your brain, head, and face.

The sixth chakra represents intuition, intellect, and wisdom.

The sixth chakra hum: *The hum is in between the eyebrows at the third eye.*

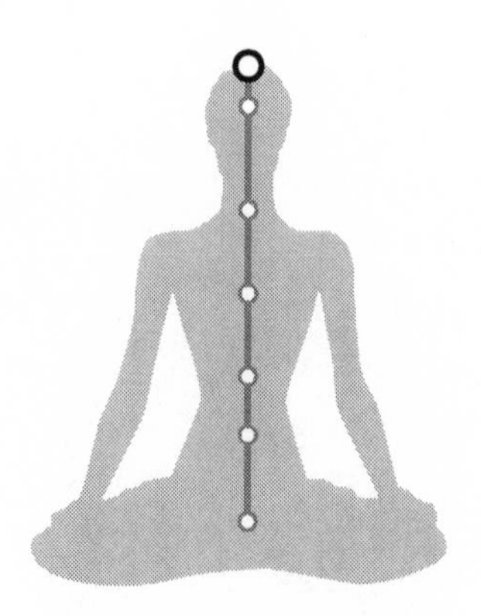

SEVENTH CHAKRA.

The crown chakra is located at the very top of the head. It represents our connection to the Universe and to our Source/The Divine/God, whatever you call that power that is bigger than yourself.

The seventh chakra is located around the scalp and skull and is related to the nervous system, as well as to the muscular system and the skin.

Through the seventh chakra, we remember that we are connected to the universal energy that powers all living things.

The seventh chakra hum: *Imagine attaching a string at the top of your head and then pulling upward, elongating your spine. Feel the energy draw up to the point where the string begins and imagine there is a geyser of energy coming out of the center point of the top of your head.*

In the next chapters, we will go more in depth into each of the seven chakras. Within each chakra chapter, you will find several thought balloons - ideas to help you create and envision scenarios and images to use for the visual part of your meditation.
Thought balloons are tagged with this button
At the end of each chakra chapter, there are workbook questions for you to think about and/or answer that may spark more ideas. Feel free to answer all of the questions or none of them - they are there for you.

Now get ready to create your personal roadmap to Elevate!

Stripped down version:

Here are the chakras and where you can find them on your body.

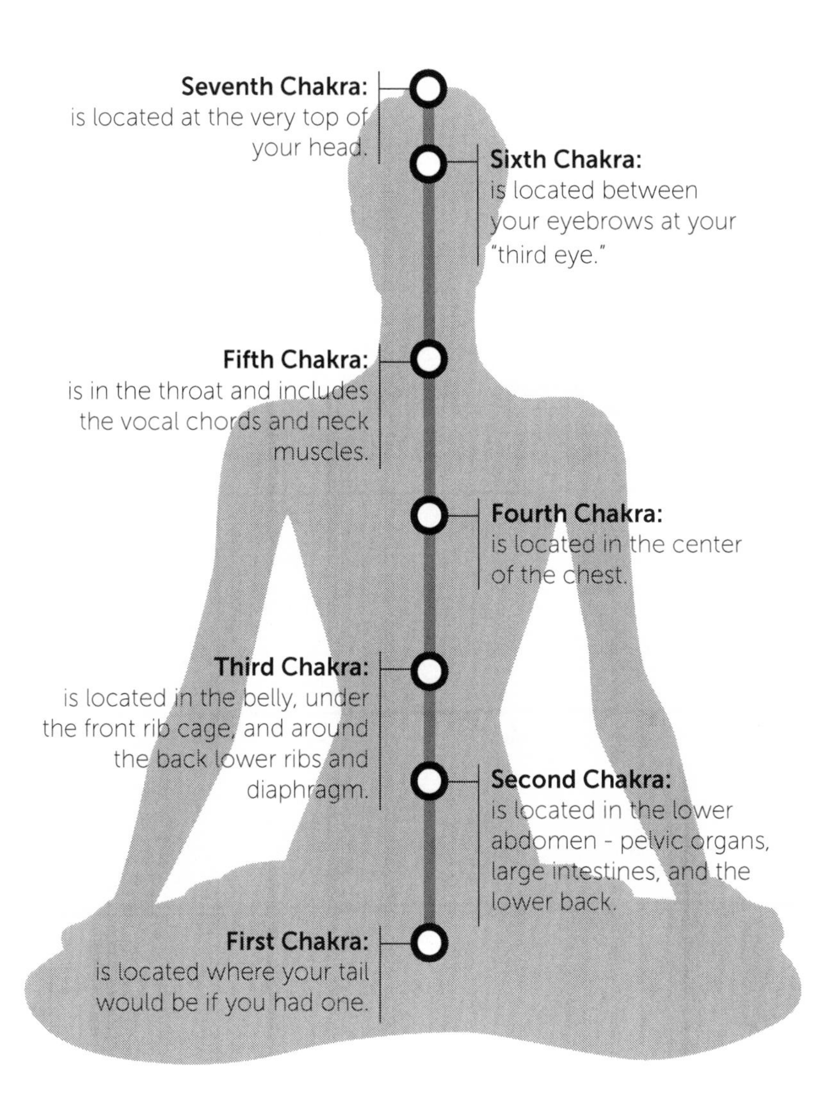
Seventh Chakra:
is located at the very top of your head.
Sixth Chakra:
is located between your eyebrows at your "third eye."
Fifth Chakra:
is in the throat and includes the vocal chords and neck muscles.
Fourth Chakra:
is located in the center of the chest.
Third Chakra:
is located in the belly, under the front rib cage, and around the back lower ribs and diaphragm.
Second Chakra:
is located in the lower abdomen - pelvic organs, large intestines, and the lower back.
First Chakra:
is located where your tail would be if you had one.

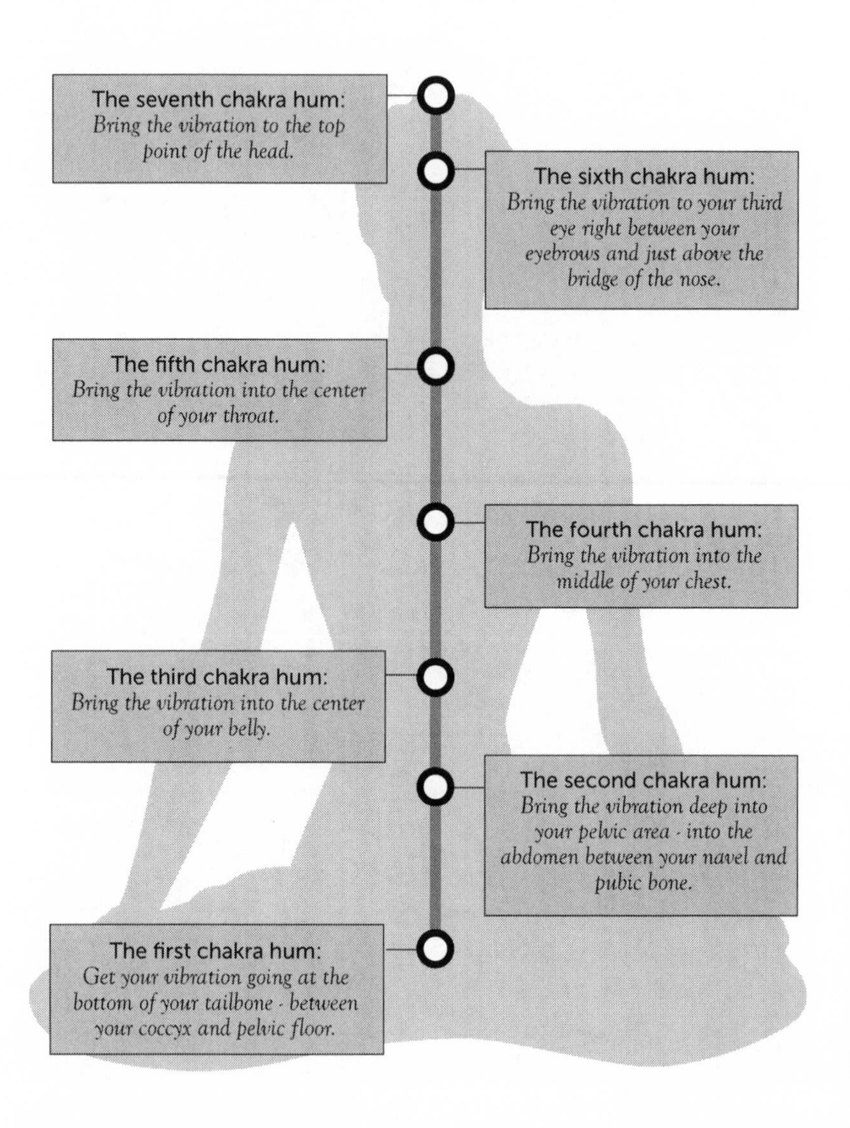
The seventh chakra hum:
Bring the vibration to the top point of the head.
The sixth chakra hum:
Bring the vibration to your third eye right between your eyebrows and just above the bridge of the nose.
The fifth chakra hum:
Bring the vibration into the center of your throat.
The fourth chakra hum:
Bring the vibration into the middle of your chest.
The third chakra hum:
Bring the vibration into the center of your belly.
The second chakra hum:
Bring the vibration deep into your pelvic area - into the abdomen between your navel and pubic bone.
The first chakra hum:
Get your vibration going at the bottom of your tailbone - between your coccyx and pelvic floor.

THE ROOT

Chakra 1

All living things have roots. A plant uses its roots to receive nutrients that it needs to grow. The roots of a tree drive down into the earth, branching out and becoming deeply embedded in the ground. The more solidly entrenched the roots are in the ground, the more robust the growing plant will be.

Human beings also have roots. Our roots are with our ancestors, our families, and our "tribes," or the people with whom we identify the most. Dr. Bruce Lipton, a developmental biologist who studies epigenetics, says that our fundamental beliefs and the way we see the world are formed in our first six years of life. This early foundation illustrates how important these roots are--made up of our parents, relatives, teachers and spiritual leaders--especially in those early years.

It is our roots that keep us anchored and supported. At the same time, it is also our roots that can limit us. *If the people who represent our roots are supportive, positive, understanding, and respectful toward us, our roots can nourish, nurture, and teach us.*

I was always a very good student and worked hard to get good grades. I grew up living with my mom in a small apartment, and we did not have much money. However, my mother's sister and her husband lived ten minutes away and had plenty of money. My uncle came from humble beginnings but by mid-life, he had become a financial success. He was a principled man with a tremendous commitment to family. My aunt and uncle helped my mother buy her apartment and helped with car payments. For me, they paid for piano lessons, summer sleepaway camps, and back-to-school clothes. The icing on the generosity cake: My aunt and uncle paid for my college education.

Since my uncle's passing in 2011, his children have maintained his estate and his generosity by running a philanthropic fund that supports organizations that do important and life-changing work around the globe. From watching my cousins, I have learned how generosity feeds us in

a special way. My aunt, uncle and cousins are tremendously positive tribal influences for me.

Another positive first chakra influence for me is my mother. My mom, like most of us, has a complicated story. She had to raise two children alone on a small income (and very bouncy child support checks from my father). On top of that, she struggled with depression for much of her life and most of my childhood. My mother was born during the Great Depression and was raised by immigrant Jewish parents who had escaped anti-Semitic Poland before most of their relatives were murdered. Like many surviving European Jews, this history was the source of some complicated emotional energy in the household. My mom grew up in a house full of survivor's guilt, on top of financial guilt, on top of an internal anxiety about where the next meal was coming from. This honest memory of the reality of suffering carried over into my mother's generation, as did the anxiety around finances.

Think of a person in your life who is a role model for the "good life," whether it's doing important work or living a lifestyle that you admire. This can be a teacher or guide; it can be your mother or father, aunt, cousin, Atticus Finch, Eleanor Roosevelt, or Stevie Wonder. The key is, it is someone who is purely positive for you. Someone who stretches the possibility for whatever you want to draw into your life. Someone you admire. Imagine that person you respect and admire giving you a gift or supporting you in some way unconditionally. Applauding your success. Looking at you with kindness and love. Standing beneath you with open arms ready to catch you when you jump.

Yet, my mother did the best she could with me and showed me tons of love. I got snuggled, cuddled, complimented, and praised. She wrote me love notes. She talked to me like an adult, even when I was a toddler. She encouraged honesty (even though as a teenager I was sometimes dishonest

Think about someone in your life who has been extremely supportive or loving to you. Picture that person, whether real or fictional. The more specific you can be, the better. The picture must be believable to you. The important part is to feel the emotional vibration associated with the picture.

with her) and communication (even though as a teenager I sometimes did not speak to her).

This is a positive first chakra emotion: Feeling loved, feeling treasured, feeling wanted by the one who brought you into this world. I am full of gratitude to my mother for encouraging me to feel all of those things. I am well aware that not everyone can say that of their parent. And I have tremendous gratitude that, at eighty-something years old, she is still here.

Another first chakra gift from my mother, and from all of the women of her generation, is the Women's Liberation movement. Women like my mother, some of whom found themselves raising children alone (as divorce became more of a viable option in the late sixties and early seventies) and some of whom were just plain bored, went out and started working. This was not easy back then; women were not exactly welcomed into the workforce. Many of them had to climb very long ladders to get into careers besides the more traditional ones of teaching, nursing, and retail. Because of my mother and her circle of women friends, I grew up with a model of what it meant to be a woman in the world doing good work. It was not a question of whether I would work, but rather a question of what I would do to make my mark on the world. This opportunity had not been the case for many women in the generations before mine.

Recently a friend of mine remarked that she feels she was misled by the Women's Lib movement of the sixties and seventies. She said that, as direct descendants of women's libbers, we were brought up to believe that women could do everything. We could have families and careers

and make it all seamless. In actuality, it is very difficult to do it all. You can have a family and a gratifying career, but you won't be able to go to every soccer game, volunteer at every field day, or head up the PTA. The message, she said, should have been "You can have anything, you just have to choose which thing you want to put the most energy into - and then feel OK about sucking at the other thing."

The positive and the negative.

Just as positive experiences and relationships can create more harmony in the first chakra, negative influences can also establish discord. When our roots are grown with disrespect, intolerance, and negativity around our lives and our choices, they can limit us. Many of our limiting beliefs about life, abundance, love, healing – what we cannot do or achieve – come from our tribal roots, our parents, ancestors, teachers, role models, and spiritual leaders.

I remember watching the movie, *Cinderella* with my daughter years ago. Cinderella would come up with some great ideas and be told, "It simply isn't done!"* How many decisions did we make as children, teens, and young adults that were informed by negative ideas that were passed down to us by our tribe? Think of how limited thinking affects generations--the perpetuation of racism, anti-semitism, homophobia, and sexism, to name a few. Think of how certain world religions have affected what a woman (or an African American or a Muslim or a transgender person... or fill in the blank) can or cannot do, how she

Think about someone in your life who has been extremely supportive or loving to you. Picture that person, whether real or fictional. The more specific you can be, the better. The picture must be believable to you. The important part is to feel the emotional vibration associated with the picture.

**To be sure that the quote was from Cinderella and not another Disney movie, I googled "it simply isn't done" and, sure enough, Cinderella popped up. The search had 231 million hits.*

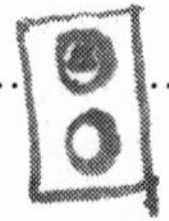

Picture being surrounded by the material things that make you feel safe. Imagine knowing and trusting that they are your things and will not be taken away or dissolved. Imagine having an infinite supply of the material things that make you feel safe and secure--money, food, a home, or anything else that gives you the feeling of stability.

can be educated or not, how she can achieve or not. When we have limits, it restricts our ability to grow.

Poverty and inequality occur largely from a national and global first chakra discord. These toxic systems have been created across generations and continents by people thinking they are superior to others and setting up patterns that transcend centuries reinforcing these patterns. The tribal nature of racism, sexism, homophobia, and intolerance for others is something that is taught early and often by our parents, teachers, and clergy. Women who are involved in relationships that are violent are often operating on the discord of their first chakra; what our tribes teach us has a lot to do with our beliefs and paradigms as we go through life. Adults who were abused as children often become abusers themselves. These are obvious damages brought on by first chakra disharmony.

There are more subtle examples of tribal discord that lead to destructive beliefs and patterns. I have many patients who were raised in households where alternative medicine and energy healing were taboo. One or both of their parents was a medical doctor or scientist. Or they themselves were trained in medicine or empirical science. In their minds, anything that could not be explained with a case-controlled research study was bunk. These are folks who have taken a long time to get to me, trying everything else under the sun first before attempting a natural, holistic, more energetic method of healing. I have to work hard to gain their trust, but when I do, they are often amazed by how a little bit of touch and a small amount of "hands-on" healing can help so tremendously.

When I was growing up, I had some relatives who were also entrenched in the medical mindset. Some of them were quite vocal about their skepticism of my career choice as a chiropractor. "Don't you want to be a *real* doctor?" they said. "Don't you want to do something worthwhile? Don't you want to be respected? Why do you want to be a quack?" I'd like to say I went forward with my choice with no hesitation, but that isn't true. After constantly hearing this rhetoric, I decided to try out medicine and worked for one year doing medical research at a top medical college in New York City. During this time, I took a class in nutrition at the med school just to try it out.

Imagine getting a letter in the mail and finding out that you are in the will of a distant relative who you don't know and that person has left you a large amount of money. See the letter. Try to read it in your mind. How much money did they leave you? Now for fun, multiply that by five or twenty or a thousand. Imagine how that feels! Make sure to see the vision on your mind's TV screen. (Don't focus on the illusion of it, otherwise you will be using your doubt and skepticism as your point of attraction, which will provide the opposite effect!)

Here's a little background: my father was a "health food nut." He was obsessed with alfalfa sprouts and whole wheat bread. When I stayed with him in the summertime, I died of embarrassment when he offered my friends brown rice cakes with seaweed or his own homemade peanut butter for a snack. In spite of my embarrassment and the discomfort of having to choke down a handful of vitamins every day of my summer vacation, I learned a lot about the healing power of food and nutrients. I knew about Adele Davis and *Prevention Magazine* before they were in vogue. My dad saw a chiropractor for wellness care before that was cool. Besides the major stash of Suzie Qs in the closet for those uncontrollable sugar cravings, my dad modeled healthy nutrition in a time when it was not on most people's radar.

Picture an ancestor or relative who is very wealthy - real or fictional, it doesn't matter. What matters is the emotion that you tie in with the image. Regardless of who this relative or ancestor is, know that there is no limit to the amount of money this person has. Imagine that this person is taking you out to dinner and is footing the bill. How do you feel looking at the menu? How does it feel to order what you truly want and as much of it as you truly want? Oysters Rockefeller? A bottle of champagne? Sixteen cheeseburgers?

During the first week of nutrition class at NYU, our lab task was to compare home-made chocolate chip cookie dough to store-bought dough (I believe it was Betty Crocker.) This wasn't the scientific class I had hoped for where I was going to learn how to change people's health through nutrition. The second week of class, we discussed electrolytes. "Oh goody," I thought, "I might actually learn something this week!" The teacher talked about how when we sweat a lot, we lose salt. Replacing large amounts of plain water when you sweat profusely can lead to an electrolyte imbalance, which can be a huge problem causing dizziness, nausea, and fainting. "Interesting," I thought. My hand shot up. "What would you recommend for someone who, let's say, is playing tennis all day and sweating?" The teacher answered, "I would just tell them to eat a bag of potato chips." I realized that I already knew more about nutrition than the teacher. I dropped the class.

The next thing I realized about myself was that I get weak at the sight of blood. Although that queasiness is a really good reason NOT to become a medical doctor, that ultimately isn't why I decided that medicine was not for me. There was a limited worldview in medicine that I already had transcended. If I were to go the medicine route, I would constantly be fighting for my own vision of health, and I didn't want to spend all of my energy that way. There are some great visionaries who went forward into

medicine, like Dr. Christiane Northrup and Dr. Andrew Weil, who have changed the landscape of complementary medicine. However, I decided that I would take my intellect and skill as a rational scientist and see how I could serve people in a more natural, holistic way.

It wasn't that I was so passionate about chiropractic and the value of good alignment for the spine and nervous system. That passion came much later, after many years in practice. It was that I wanted to serve others and needed a good shingle to put outside as a springboard for my work. And yet, with some of my goals more clearly defined, I still walked into the profession feeling like a second class citizen. I was in practice for over ten years before I started to change my professional self-esteem. And I know my low self-worth was all because of those roots--the chatter that started when I was young and my relatives who told me I was too good for chiropractic. They told me Western medicine was superior, and therefore was the only field for any self-respecting, smart person.

There was also a first chakra tribal money issue for me. My mother was a counselor and my father was a college professor. All of their friends were teachers, social workers, and artists. My parents' demographic seemed to shared a common belief that doing good work and making money could not coexist. There was a contradiction in that generation from growing up with no money and scarcity because of world events, war, the Depression, yet at the same time feeling that money is the root of all evil. Therefore, they believed if you are doing good work in the world, you should not make good money because that would be greedy. And with so many people in the world who had no money, it would be unfair for you to have it. That's a root I needed to work very hard to pull out of the ground.

The post-script of the story is that it is possible to rise above those deep-rooted paradigms, but it takes work. Jon Kabat Zinn says, "None of us has to be a helpless victim of what was done to us or what was not done for us in the past, nor do we have to be helpless in the face of what we may be suffering now. We are also what was present before the scarring – our original wholeness, what was born whole. And we

can reconnect with that intrinsic wholeness at any time, because its very nature is that it is always present. It is who we truly are." Being as present with yourself as you can be, celebrating the roots that hold you up, and creating new roots with friendship and love – that is what is possible for healing and cherishing this aspect of your life.

Workbook Questions and Ideas for the First Chakra.

Answer the questions that are relative to you. You can answer as many or as few questions as you want. The goal is to isolate an easy and accessible image for the first chakra visualization. Remember, you can change your image any time you wish – every day, if you like. But this is where you start. Or you can use these suggestions as a template for other questions.

Who are the role models in your life?

Why do you consider them role models?

Is there someone in your life who has been generous to you, either in word, deed, or from the heart?

What does happiness look like, and who taught you about that?

What does unconditional love mean to you, and do you have someone in your life who represents that for you – living, dead, or fictional?

What material things make you feel safe and secure? What material things do you need in your life to be happy, to feel
no fear?

Who taught you about material things?

What are the material things that you would like more of?

What would it feel like to have an infinite supply of that thing?

How would having more of that thing change your life in a positive way?

Uplifting Ideas

Suggestions for the first chakra image:

When you are thinking about your first chakra image, choose pictures that give you a feeling of harmony, happiness, and abundance. Choose pictures of ancestors, members of your tribe, people in your life whom you hold in high regard. Choose what makes you feel grounded and whole.

Here are some suggestions for uplifting ideas for your first chakra Elevate image:

- Someone who is a role model, whom you admire
- Someone who supports you unconditionally
- Someone with open arms ready to catch you when you jump
- A generous person treating you to something luxurious
- Getting a letter that informs you of an unexpected financial bonus
- Being surrounded by things that make you feel safe and happy

Whether you are using one of these uplifting images, or coming up with an idea of your own, choose an image that you can conjure quickly. Write a brief description of the image you have selected.

THE SOIL: PLANTING SEEDS

Chakra 2

In order for a seed to grow effectively, it needs good, nutritious, fertile soil. Here is where the seed is sown. A fertile place is what creates new plants, new life, and new ideas. The soil feeds the seed to promote its development and supports the seed while it grows.

In life, we get ideas – those proverbial light bulbs above our heads – and then nurture our ideas with our thoughts and actions until they come to fruition, just as seeds one day will literally bear fruit. This is the second chakra, or energy level, of the body: the seed of creation. The second chakra is our creative center, our soil. This area, located in the lower abdomen (an area which has the potential to create life), represents our ability to produce new ideas that lead to producing new things. Everything that is now in our lives was once a thought. When we get in our cars to go to work in the morning, we don't usually stop and think about the person who originally said, "Hmm... I wonder if humans will ever move from place to place on a machine with wheels." That idea was created from an original thought. It needed support in order to grow and flourish into action, and then it became
a reality.

Think of a creative project you have felt drawn to. *It might be a work of art, a book, a music album, or a band you started. If you are a musician, do you see yourself writing music for other people? Or performing solo? Creating an album or video? Do you want to join with other musicians? Where would be your dream place to perform? Are you a poet? A dancer? A sculptor? A painter?*

Metaphysically, the second chakra is connected to the three big life issues: power, sex, and money. Stresses in those three areas (who doesn't have stress in at least one of those?) can have a profound effect on the body. For instance, many people carry their money stress in their lower back. Of course, as a chiropractor, lower back pain is one of the conditions I see the most. For some of these folks, just getting them to make the

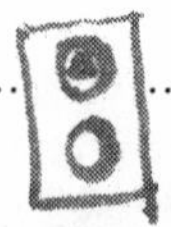

Look at the book cover; imagine yourself holding a copy of your newly published book. See yourself opening the envelope with the cash advance (for your next book) from the company that just published you.

connection and think (really think) about money and their relationship with it can help them become free from their pain. Sometimes it literally works like magic.

Bill: When I was newly in practice, I had a patient, Bill, who suffered from acute lower back pain. I adjusted him for several weeks, but he did not improve in the way I had expected. At the time, I was starting to learn about the chakras and their connection to physical health issues. So I sat down with him and explained the relationship between lower back and financial stress. I said, "I know this sounds crazy, but have you been having financial issues lately?" His eyes grew wide, and he began to tell me how his business had all of a sudden started to do poorly and how he was afraid that it was going to fail. He expressed some deep feelings to me in that session, even got teary. Over the course of the next few visits, his symptoms improved dramatically and he started to feel more like his old self. It wasn't so much the actual business itself that caused his physical problem, but his perception and fear around the issue that seemed to be contributing to his pain.

The Lost Idea: Think of how many ideas you have had that you haven't ever recorded, acted upon, or brought to fruition. You could go crazy – if you let yourself – trying to capture every single good idea that floats into your mind. But where do these ideas come from? When do they happen? How do you know a good idea when you think of one? What should you do when you notice one? And what are the consequences of letting one slip by?

For me, these good ideas can come at any time and at any moment, especially when I am the least prepared to write them down. I also know

that my blasts of inspiration that contain those good ideas, the most worthy ones, arrive when I am at my most grounded. When I am eating well and not ingesting too much sugar, caffeine, or alcohol. When I am exercising regularly. When I am getting enough good sleep. When I am meditating regularly, even for a few minutes each day. This is the state when I am the most receptive to my creative thoughts, those seeds that lead me to great ideas. That's not to say that they don't happen when I am a slug on the couch eating brownies. Regardless, my motto is "be prepared." The key, really, is to be mindful of new ideas. Notice them and make the effort to record them, even if it means getting out of bed in the wee hours of the morning to find a pencil.

I don't carry around notecards, or a pad and pen, but many people do so they can write down ideas as they occur. I often get insights when I'm in the shower, in the woods on a hike with my dog, or while driving down the highway – all very inconvenient moments. And as I careen into my sixth decade of life*, I find that my memory is not what it used to be. If I have an idea when I'm pulling my car into the garage, I'll need to repeat it over and over again in a cadence (sometimes sung to a tune) in order to remember it all the way into the house. "I must call mom, call my mom, call my mom...." Then, once I'm in the house, I am greeted by my dog who is so fabulously excited to see me that I'll completely forget what it was I was repeating, and then it becomes a lost idea.

Sometimes the lost ideas return, but many times they don't. Thus, I have become adept with the voice memo app on my phone so I can record ideas. This method is easy and convenient, as long as I remember to keep my phone charged and remember to check my voice memos at the end of the day. Thank goodness I have the Reminders app for that!

**At the time of this writing, I am 50 years old. I gasped audibly when I realized that it is my sixth decade that has just started, not my fifth.*

Develop a positive picture in your mind of something you would like to create. Think about why you want to create it. If it is a creation that you hope to someday get paid for, think about (and visualize) the money coming in because of that creation. More importantly, imagine what emotions you will feel as money comes in because of that creation.

If you envision ideas as little balloons, imagine how many little balloons there are floating around out there. For some people, the idea is about the next big project; something that will help get an important message out to the world. For some it's about a personal creative endeavor – their next painting, poem, work of art, novel, or song. Or it could be an idea about finding or improving a relationship or about expanding productivity in a business, a new business venture or a new marketing direction. For others, the idea could be about attracting more abundance and wealth.

When a strong idea comes along and we pay attention to it – really devoting our energy and intention – this can lead to some very enriching and sometimes surprising opportunities. Who do we run into on the street that same day? What message do we happen to hear on the radio? What article randomly arrives in our inbox or on Facebook? These kinds of experiences, the hair-raising ones, are often called coincidences. But there is more order to the Universe than we think.

I was five years into my chiropractic career when I got pregnant with my first child. When she was born, I continued to work several days a week seeing patients. The truth was, I was exhausted in every way. Eventually, after reviewing our finances and seeing that somehow we would be able to squeak by on one income, my husband and I decided that I would stay at home with the baby rather than paying for daycare at the expense of my own health. My daughter did not sleep through the night until she was four years old, so I spent quite a few years literally walking around like a

zombie. Still, I knew how lucky I was to be given this gift of time with my daughter. She and I became a duo spending every day together, navigating the terrain of our new home, Boston, and meeting other parents who had babies and dogs. We had a posse that would walk around Fresh Pond every morning and then retire to the coffee shop for playing with the other children and gabbing with the other adults. It was a good life.

Your goal in designing this creation may be to improve your reputation, recognition, status, or to win some sort of award or race. If so, then make that finishing line your image and conjure the emotion that comes from achieving that goal. Create the whole picture.

And then (cue the scary music) child number two arrived. I was so grateful to get pregnant again, and grateful to the Universe for providing us with a son, who I cherish like any good Jewish mother would (he's so nice and so handsome). In addition, I would never want to scare anyone off from having multiple children; it is perhaps the greatest gift of all. However, it was a game-changer to have two kids. I could not catch up on sleep; they both woke at different times of the night, requiring my intervention in different ways. They were also on different nap schedules. My son hated anything having to do with motion, including the car, the stroller, or the baby-carrier, and would only stop crying if he was held and bounced. The addition of this new child took exhaustion to a new level and included some depression in the mix. I found myself grumpy all the time, wanting to pull my hair out, craving adult companionship. My only identity was becoming "MOMMYYYYYY," the parent of young children, and not "Dr.", the professional I once was. I knew without a doubt it was time to go back to work.

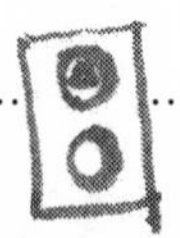

Stand at the podium in Norway and accept your Nobel Prize. Stand on the stage at the Metropolitan Opera and gaze out at the audience giving you a standing ovation. Cross the finish line of the Boston Marathon. Feel the burn. Feel the exhilaration. Feel proud of yourself. What does that look and feel like?

The second I realized it, I felt my mood lift. I began to visualize the creation of my chiropractic office. I saw what my office would look like, the perfect location, how I would decorate it, and what hours I would hold. I even picked paint colors for the as yet non-existent walls of my office. The amazing thing was that once the visualizing was in motion, opportunities started coming in almost faster than I could handle them. After looking at a few not-perfect spaces for lease, an office opened up around the corner from my house. It was light and airy, on the main street, and had plenty of parking in the back. The rent was affordable. I easily procured a business loan. I found the perfect chiropractic tables at a used equipment store, both in the purple color I had picked for my color scheme. I also found a desk at a discount furniture store, and the guy on the phone literally said to me, "So sorry, we only have this desk left in purple." It was like the second I made the decision in my heart and got my emotions around it, the Universe dropped a flood of opportunities upon me.

Five years later, well-entrenched in my practice and finding a manageable balance in my work-family life, my husband and I decided that we were growing out of our small starter home and began to look for a bigger house. We started by trying to make our one hundred year-old house bigger, but that venture proved to be nothing but a headache. Apparently our floors were slanted (who knew?) and putting on an addition would be nearly impossible. Because we were in an affluent town in the Boston suburbs, trying to find a bigger home was proving to be an expensive endeavor, too pricey for our budget. We put the idea to rest.

Imagine starting a new business venture, a political campaign, or a hedge fund. Imagine the outcome of a successful project.

My husband did, at least. I began visualizing my perfect home. I thought about the features of the home I wanted. I thought about the color of the outside of the house. I visualized and visualized (as I will mention later in another chapter) and, lo and behold, the perfect house literally dropped into our laps! Because of the way we found the house, I was sure the Universe was in on it and that it was meant to be, and there were many reasons why. The house wasn't even on the market yet when we found out about it. The next door neighbor was crazy about dogs and immediately fell in love with Ginger, our chocolate lab. We found we had many interests and people in common with many of our potential new neighbors. One of them, a music producer, had done some recording in Nashville a few years back. We had lived in Nashville in the 90s and, as musicians ourselves, had sung on a friend's album as a favor to him. It turned out that this neighbor was the producer on THAT album! The coincidences kept coming.

We made a bid on the house that we were sure was ours, and that night we celebrated. That is, until the phone rang at 9:00. It was the owner of the house; someone else had bid higher at the last minute. I was flabbergasted! This was so definitely my house! How could they think about selling it to another family? My husband and I pondered many different scenarios--should we put in a higher bid (with money we didn't have) or should we back off? My vision was so strong about this house that I really couldn't imagine a world where it was not ours. We decided to trust in the process, trust in the Universe, and sleep on it. The next morning, as I was about to dial his number to negotiate, the owner called me and told me that the other buyer's funding fell through and the house was ours! I breathed a sigh of relief, fist-bumped my husband, and knew that the right thing had indeed happened.

The Universal Laws say there is no such thing as coincidence. Energy is energy. It cannot be created or destroyed. The energy of an idea, according to law, will attract elements and opportunities with similar vibration. When you get a great idea – especially if you become emotionally attached or excited about it – things will happen. Sometimes those things can blow your mind.

In order to see an idea come into existence as a reality, you have to take action. But when you are emotionally super-charged about the idea, the actions often seem to fall into place easily.

Imagine yourself taking action on an idea and feeling joy in it. *What are the actions that make you feel excitement?*

Sometimes it is not that easy. Sometimes it feels like you can't get the break, can't land the job, the partner – you keep missing the mark. Marianne Williamson once said, "If the train does not stop at your station, it is not your train." When it feels like you are not receiving opportunities, or the ones you are getting are not filling you up, maybe it's a good idea to re-think what it is you are emotionally attached to. Are you focused on having the opportunity or not-having the opportunity? It can make a big difference. And sometimes you are waiting for a train that really isn't yours. Is the opportunity really what you want deep down in your heart?

There is always risk involved with creativity. Sometimes it isn't enough to just have the idea and take the action. So much of the time we get bogged down by the fear of failure, and our creative juices stop flowing. Our inner critic can be very loud, and it is easy for that rascal to convince us that we aren't good enough or smart or worthy enough. In order to keep the second chakra open, we must move through that fear and trust in the action. Know that we have an infinite amount of creative energy and, if it doesn't fly this time, we can always try again. With this meditation, we can bring more energy into the lower abdomen, and thus be more free to create.

Workbook Questions and Ideas for the Second Chakra.

Answer the questions that are relative to you. You can answer as many or as few questions as you want. The goal is to isolate an easy and accessible image for the second chakra visualization. Remember, you can change your image any time you wish.

If you are an artist, or aspire to be one, what is your medium?

Where would you like to do your creating?

What would you like to accomplish with your creations?

How do you imagine your creations will affect people?

Have you ever started your own business?

Are you an entrepreneur?

Do you have an invention?

Do you have an idea for a business that could be the next best thing?

Are you in a relationship?

Do you want to attract a new relationship?

Does it bring you joy? What other feelings does it bring up for you?

What are the relationships in your life that make you happy?

Is there something about a specific relationship that you would like to change?

What are your goals for relationship with others?

Uplifting Ideas

Suggestions for the second chakra image:

When you are thinking about your second chakra image, choose pictures that represent creativity. Choose pictures that make you feel productive, powerful, successful, or abundant.

Here are some suggestions for uplifting ideas for your second chakra Elevate image:

- A finished creative project: a CD, a book, a piece of artwork
- Imagine the project coming to life - feel the accomplishment, see the standing ovation, hear the applause
- The birth of a successful new business venture
- Winning an award for your skill, talent or product

Whether you are using one of these uplifting images, or coming up with an idea of your own, choose an image that you can conjure quickly. Write a brief description of the image you have selected.

THE CENTER

Chakra 3

We have arrived at the third level of energy, also known as the *solar plexus*. The third chakra is located in the belly. To clarify, although belly and stomach are words often used interchangeably, the stomach is an organ that lies right under your rib cage slightly to the left of center. But when we say "Put your hand on your belly," we are really talking about the third chakra.

This is the home of the ego. This is the energy center that determines who we are, how we see ourselves, and how we feel about ourselves. *This chakra encompasses our self-esteem and our self-image. Are we worthy of love, success, happiness, and peace?*

Since the third chakra is related to its neighbor, the second chakra, it makes sense that self-esteem and self-worth become intrinsically connected to the creative process. When there is a creative seed expressed as an idea and a project comes to life, a tremendous sense of self-worth can emerge. Sometimes a project that starts with a great idea and has momentum ends up not coming into being. Sometimes we are unable to see a project through to its completion. When this happens, our energies get blocked, either from feeling let down by ourselves or frustrated by life not moving forward as we had imagined it could. This struggle can create havoc in our self-esteem and make us feel crappy about ourselves.

The ego is also connected to the first chakra – where our beliefs about ourselves originated from being taught by the people who came before us – and to the fourth chakra, which is our ability to love others and ourselves.

The organs that are associated with the third chakra include the stomach, liver, gall bladder, adrenal glands, and small intestines. Digestive disorders are more prevalent in our society than any other ailment. Stress-related ulcers, IBS, constipation, and reflux are ubiquitous (as well as gallstones, liver disease, and adrenal fatigue as a result of living in the "fight or flight"

part of our nervous systems 24/7). These illnesses and conditions are all chakra three.

See how it feels to look at yourself and smile with appreciation and love? Picture saying "I love you" to yourself and feeling totally normal about it. Take a step further and imagine feeling really good about it.

These common health "epidemics" may be due, in part, to a culture in which we are not expected to fully love ourselves. In fact, it seems in many ways more en vogue to put ourselves down. Self-deprecating humor and reality TV are what sells in the media. Think about *The Bachelor*, an embarrassingly and morbidly appealing TV show which highlights a bunch of women who each try to get one man to fall in love with her. Throughout the show, we see each woman fall apart one by one and walk away with her tail tucked between her legs, rejected and hurt. She is crying or bawling. This is entertainment in America, creating an environment where it is normal for us (especially women) to feel we are not enough and therefore not worthy of the love and esteem of someone else. If a contestant on *The Bachelor* talked about the importance of loving herself, she would probably be thrown off the show. Whereas self-hatred is entertaining, self-love does not sell. In our culture, self-love is seen as weird, braggy, and awkward.

A strong third chakra means a strong sense of self. It doesn't mean to inflate one's idea of self beyond reality, nor does it mean to be selfish. It is often difficult for us to love ourselves. We have trouble allowing our own love into our lives. In her book *You Can Heal Your Life*, Louise Hay suggests the exercise of looking in the mirror, deep into your own eyes, and saying out loud, "I love you." It's fascinating how constantly we all look in the mirror but how rarely we look – really look – deep into our own eyes. It's hard to do at first without feeling like a complete creep (maybe better to do it when no one is around).

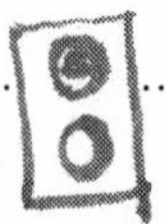

Picture what you look like at your most generous. Are you writing checks to charity? Are you surprising someone with an unexpected tip? Are you lovingly giving a gift to a friend?

Like many emotions, self-love is like a muscle. It can be very weak at first and can feel awkward to flex. But with practice, you can develop a stronger self-esteem that can strengthen your relationships with others (and yourself) as well as your ability to create and make an impact on the world around you. Improving your self-esteem will also help with your vibration. Seeing yourself as someone of great worth makes you vibrate as someone of great worth. That vibration will attract elements worthy of a person of great worth.

Marco Third chakra weakness and lack of self-esteem are often caused by fear. A patient of mine, Marco, recently experienced an epiphany about how fear has been holding him back in his life. He was on a trip with a few dads and their teenage boys. The weekend was full of fun and games. However, on the last day of the trip, the group planned a day of white water rafting, something Marco had never done before. He actually found the idea terrifying and couldn't imagine himself doing it. As a kid, he had suffered with a fear of the water; it took him years to learn how to swim and still, at age fifty-five, when faced with the idea of being submerged under water, he reverted to his old fears and panicky feelings. He planned to leave early before the rafting trip started and explained to the other guys (and his son) that he really needed to work that day and couldn't go rafting.

As he pulled away from the group to start the long drive home, he felt badly about himself. His self-esteem was in the toilet, and he realized that he was modeling fear-based behavior for his son, who was going to be rafting solo with the other boys and their dads. He tried to brush it off and stopped at a diner for some coffee. He decided to download a podcast to

listen to on the drive. He had recently heard about *On Being, with Krista Tippett,* a podcast of interviews about life and spirituality. He mindlessly went to the first episode he could find (think Wheel of Fortune-type selection process) and started listening.

It just so happened that what he randomly downloaded was an interview with Craig Minowa, a songwriter who writes incredibly deep lyrics about finding the magic in life, God, fear and courage. There was one line in particular that stood out to Marco: 'The most important thing that makes us human is courage.' Minowa also spoke a lot about finding holiness in the wilderness. Marco was already halfway home when he decided to turn the car around. He put the address of the rafting center into his GPS, and he found he had exactly enough time to make it before the boys and the other dads went into the water – literally the exact number of minutes! On the drive to the river, he vowed that he would find holiness in that wilderness and make each moment count instead of succumbing to his fear and trying to get through the experience as quickly as possible. He was determined to conquer his fear of the water and "man up". He wanted to model courage for his son. He felt his life shift when he made the decision to go back, and he felt a profound change in his self-esteem. That is hard third chakra work!

Marco was in a boat with a few boys and a few dads and one leader. When the boat would hit some rapids, the leader would shout, "Use your core! Use your core!" to remind the group to engage the abdominal and core muscles to help them stabilize in the boat. What a perfect metaphor for Marco in that moment, as he was totally working the third chakra inside and out!

How we are seen by others. The third chakra can also relate to concern about how others see you. A weakness in the third chakra around self-worth may inadvertently define how you see yourself by how you perceive others to feel about you. There is great value in always acting with kindness and taking actions that are for the greater good, essentially

being a good person who does good work. But our worth also arises from within us and around us.

George. I wanted to do a small construction project in our house. I called a local contractor and scheduled a time for him to come over and give me an estimate. As I've mentioned, my memory isn't what it used to be, so I put the appointment in my calendar and set an alert for myself. The morning of the appointment, I knew he was coming. I started my morning as usual, but then my son missed his bus and asked me to drive him to school. When I dropped him off, I thought, 'Wow, I'm halfway to the gym! I should just go work out and get it over with." In the moment, I totally forgot about the carpenter. Brain fart. When I finished working out, I saw that there was a message on my phone from the carpenter, and my heart sank. I started beating myself up mentally. "I am the worst. I can't believe I stood him up. I have a horrible memory. I can't be trusted." All of these negative self-thoughts were flooding into my mind. I physically felt badly, nauseated, face flushed, and my heart felt heavy.

All of a sudden, I stopped myself. I'm not sure what did it, but it suddenly hit me that I was disappointed in myself for not being perfect. I stood the guy up, yes, but it wasn't the end of the world. This was a reaction not based in reality, but it was all about how I wanted others to see me. I had constructed a world where this act, my simple screw-up, carried enough potential to destroy another human being. I said out loud to myself, "Shit happens, Nina. You are a good person. You made a mistake." I breathed through the bad feelings and started to feel better. A few minutes into that ass-whipping-turned-to-self-love, the guy called. I answered the phone and told the truth with humility and humor. "George, I'm so sorry. I was anticipating meeting you, and then my son missed his bus, and I completely forgot about you. Like, my brain went poof and our appointment never existed." George laughed heartily and said, "No problem, Nina. That happens to me all the time! Thanks for being so honest." It turned out to be a non-issue. It was my choice whether to put that low self-esteem out there as the point of attraction or to change it

and vibrate higher. When I made that choice, the result was immediate.

Imagine looking at yourself in the mirror, dressed in an outfit that makes you look distinguished, confident, hip, or just plain hot.

When we vibrate in a place of low self-esteem, the world is more difficult to navigate. We are more at odds with other people because we are more at odds with ourselves. And ironically, even for people with a relatively healthy self-esteem in some areas, there is something about our expectation of our own perfection that sets up a negative vibration. Putting that expectation out into the world and being disappointed again and again (because – guess what – no one is perfect) will come back to us as stress or those stressful elements we attract. Part of this meditation process is about thinking it through and, at times, when appropriate, accepting ourselves as imperfect. Letting go of the attachment to perfection can free us and ultimately change the course of our day. This is what the story of George the carpenter is all about.

Hosers. Over the last few decades, a group of my close friends have created a ritual of keeping track of our imperfections. We call them "hoser-moves". To be a hoser, in this particular group of people, is an honor and a privilege and not something about which to be ashamed. Hoser-moves vary in silliness, seriousness, and financial burden. For instance, withdrawing 200 dollars from an ATM machine and walking away without actually taking the money is a simple and understandable mistake, but proves to be a relatively expensive hoser-move. Using your wallet as a computer mouse for a few seconds is a harmless hoser-move – that is, unless fearing that your computer is broken because the mouse is "unresponsive," you then bring it to the Apple store. This becomes a more expensive mistake. Dropping your phone in the toilet is one problem. Flushing it down the toilet is a whole other problem and way more expensive. Hiding in the bushes in the middle of the night for one whole hour after you hear an intruder outside your house, only to realize it was

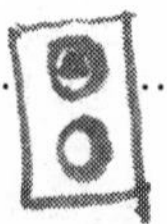

See a dinner party that others have made in your honor. Hear the glasses clink as people toast to you. (Hopefully it is a big group of hosers!)

the paper delivery man, is a hoser-move. Making what you thought was a left turn onto a street, only to realize it was a set of stairs – and continuing to drive down them – is a brilliant hoser-move. Drinking something out of a bottle on your friend's porch, thinking it was their home-brewed beer only to find out that it was petroleum solvent, is a life-threatening hoser-move. I will come clean (so to speak) and admit that for my recent (and very first) colonoscopy, I was told to drink the prep drink at 6:00, but at 6:00 I was just getting ready to leave work. I decided to drink the prep drink at work and then start my 35 minute commute. For some reason, I was convinced the prep took two hours to start working. In real life it takes far less time to start working. Let's just say I hit a traffic jam and was in a delicate, and quite imperfect, situation. Hoser-moves illustrate that in certain contexts imperfection reigns. It's all about your attitude. (To all the hosers responsible for the moves listed above, you know who you are, and you have my utmost respect and love.)

There are many ways to raise your third chakra energy. Practice, as I've mentioned, can be very helpful. Be outwardly loving to yourself. Forgive yourself for not being perfect and honor your inner hoser. Love your love handles! (My husband once wrote a country song called *Can Your Love Handle My Love Handles?*) Be grateful that you are human.

When I talked to George the carpenter after the missed appointment, I was grateful that I was able to change my outlook to one more of humor than humiliation. We are all human and come with imperfections, foibles, and funny moments. We can appreciate all of them and how they weave intrinsically with our perfections and good attributes, those of which we are proud and with which we are pleased.

Serving. Another way to raise your third chakra vibration is to perform service. There is nothing like serving another human being, or the planet, or the animal kingdom, to make you feel greater worth. It's a good antidote for sorrow of any kind to feel like you are benefiting someone else's life and giving to the world.

Imagine changes that have come about because of your service. Imagine people appreciating you for something important you have accomplished, for the ways in which you have served the community and humanity.

As a member of a Jewish community, I occasionally participate in Torah (Bible) study. There is a passage in the *Book of Numbers* where Moses orders the people to take apart the Tabernacle (the movable temple) they have constructed for their journey through the desert. The people need to be able to have a sacred place to worship as they wander. Most of the tribes are given carts and oxen to carry the planks and beams and heavy drapes that make up the movable structure. But the tribe of high priests is ordered to carry the sacred objects on their shoulders. No oxen, no cart. At first glance, this demand seems unfair. Why would Moses expect that these folks be able to carry around the heavy Ark of the Covenant, which includes the stone tablets with the Commandments, for hundreds of miles on their shoulders in the desert? The rabbis explain that this act is the hard work of holiness. The high priests know it because they know their self-worth, and hence they take on the task of carrying the Torah because they know the Torah – the holiness and wisdom contained in it – is what carries them. That is what service is: Some of it is arduous, some of it is boring and laborious, some of it seems mundane, but it is all holy and brings us closer to the divine and to our true selves. This is the third chakra, too.

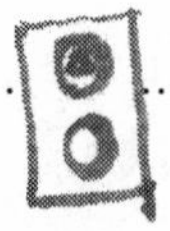

Imagine someone coming to you for advice and being inspired by your words. Imagine yourself generous, worldly, intellectual and wise. A role model admired by others. Imagine receiving your doctoral degree and being highly regarded in your field. Imagine your diploma hanging on the wall.

Our self esteem is often tied to circumstances in our lives – acknowledgment from others, how others see us. But what is most important is that we see ourselves as the best that we can be. Without judgment, and with lots of love and humor.

Workbook Questions and Ideas for the Third Chakra.

Note: Sometimes envisioning self-esteem is difficult. This exercise can feel awkward to imagine in your own mind. I encourage you to push through the awkwardness and try it. Supporting good self-esteem does not mean being boastful about yourself. The idea is to raise your positive vibration about yourself, even if you have to fake it at first. Sometimes it is easier to imagine yourself in a better materialistic situation – more money, nicer clothes – than to imagine yourself with higher self-esteem, which can be hard to visualize. Another strategy is to practice the Louise Hay exercise described in this chapter before focusing on your third chakra image.

Answer the questions that are relative to you. You can answer as many or as few questions as you want. The goal is to isolate an easy and accessible image for the third chakra visualization. Remember, you can change your image any time you wish – every day if you like.

What does it look like to have good, healthy self-esteem?

When you imagine yourself in high esteem, do you imagine yourself as you are? Or different?

When you are feeling good about yourself does it change the way others see you?

When you are feeling fit and healthy does it change how you feel about yourself? Why?

Does your appearance affect how you feel about yourself? Why? What clothing makes you feel positive about yourself? What activities? What circumstances?

Is there someone in your life that seems to have good self-esteem? What are things you have in common?

What are the ways in which you see yourself as perfect? What are your healthy imperfections? Can you imagine letting go of the negative thoughts around them?

Uplifting Ideas

Suggestions for the third chakra image:

When you are thinking about your third chakra image, choose pictures that give you a feeling of happiness, inspiration and pride about yourself.

Here are some suggestions for uplifting ideas for your third chakra Elevate image:

- Saying "I love you" to your face in the mirror - and feeling good about it
- Attending a dinner party in your honor
- You at your most generous
- Being honored for doing good work
- Getting a diploma
- Someone asking for (and wanting) your advice

Whether you are using one of these uplifting images, or coming up with an idea of your own, choose an image that you can conjure quickly. Write a brief description of the image you have selected.

THE HEART

Chakra 4

The fourth chakra represents the heart: love, compassion and forgiveness. We do not need a whole lot of background to understand the heart. It's the heart. It's the place from which love emanates.

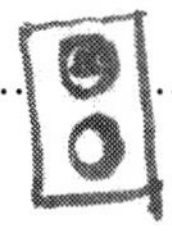

Here is an easy exercise to feel the heart chakra. Close your eyes and think of someone you love deeply. The feeling is in the middle of the chest, an expansion, a tingling, a lightness. This is the heart chakra. Think about that person (or animal), the qualities of that person that make you feel the emotion of love. Then hold the picture and feel it!

How strange it is that the source of love is an oddly-shaped, fist-sized muscle-pump that sits on the left side of our rib cage and automatically squirts blood through our vessels? Like the stomach, the actual heart organ sits on the left side of the body, but the feelings associated with it are right in the center of the chest. The heart is a perfect example of our remarkably high-tech human design; it is neurologically hard-wired to function 24/7 with no need for our conscious control. It is self-regulating with checks and balances in place to make adjustments, whether we are doing something strenuous or we are still. It responds to changes in environment and hormonal release (like if we hear a loud noise and our fight-or-flight response gets triggered). Yet, the human heart is intrinsically and viscerally connected with the emotion of love. Scientists and cardiologists know that many heart pathologies are associated with intense stress, conflict around relationships, loss, and feelings of betrayal and abandonment. There is even something called "Broken Heart Syndrome," a potentially fatal event with all the physiological changes of a heart attack (dramatic fluctuations in heart rhythm and biochemistry) but no evidence of artery blockage.

All You Need is Love. True, pure, uncomplicated love feels good. Whether it's the love of a lover, partner, child, parent, friend or pet, it all vibrates at an extremely high frequency. We all need love. Our world needs much more of it.

In the aftermath of the 2016 mass shooting at a gay nightclub in Orlando, Florida, Rabbi Darby Leigh, of Concord, Massachusetts, sent out an email to his entire congregation. He wrote:

> "So how do we respond? What do we do when we feel paralyzed? First we mourn, we express our anger and our pain... At the same time, all of us should choose love. Be love. Find a way, right now, to increase love in this world, stretch your heart, reach out, connect, and remind yourself and each other that we are in this together and that we collectively choose the path of light and of love. How long before Love and Connection truly trump Hate and Fear?"

In the wake of a violent tragedy or a natural disaster, people pour love into the world. They come together to raise money, donate blood, work at shelters, and help their sisters and brothers. It is a profound human reaction to want to help those in need during those times. It is a beautiful thing. There is unity and acceptance and love.

After 9/11 we saw America, as a community, come together for the first time in my lifetime. There was fundraising, community building, art, and music. Bruce Springsteen wrote "The Rising," an anthem in honor of the first responders. R&B performers got together and produced a telethon which raised money for the families of those who lost their lives. But most importantly, there was a feeling of unity in America (albeit very short-lived) between Red states and Blue states, Democrats and Republicans, people who voted for George W. Bush, and people who didn't vote for George W. Bush. For a time, we were all one; we were all in it together. And that is a very human reaction.

Sadly, other human reactions rose up to overtake the outpouring of love – hatred and fear. Like it is human for us to care about others, it is also very human for us to demonize people who are "others". Post 9/11, we have seen the rise of divisiveness, hatred and intolerance, war and discord in the world. In the 2016 election season, this hatred intensified to an even greater degree. Parts of America were exposed that had been bubbling underground for decades, even centuries. There was great hatred based in fear, resentment and xenophobia. As ugly as it was, it was time to pull the covers off, and bring the issues to the surface. It became clear that Americans needed to try and find compassion and understanding for one another.

As humans, we have a terrific hunger for the morbid, the evil and the terrifying. Take a look at our entertainment and media. The most popular TV shows and movies are about crime, serial killers, terrorists, zombies, and horror. What happened to *Eight is Enough*, *All in the Family* and *The Love Boat*? It is also obvious from watching the nightly news that bad news sells and good news doesn't. Sometimes on my morning commutes, I find myself yelling at the radio, "ISN'T THERE ANY GOOD NEWS??" I don't want to start my day hearing about a group of people (Americans or terrorists) who hate me (for being a Jew AND a woman!), kids with guns terrorizing their schoolmates, and the melting icebergs. We have a need to know about what is happening in the world, but there is no balance. Where is the good news?

I have often fantasized about creating an entire TV network devoted to good news. Think of how uplifting it would be to come home from a busy day at work, turn on the television and watch humans doing amazing things and being nice to each other. With the Law of Vibration being what it is – a Universal Law – if every person watched a show like that every night, we would collectively attract very different elements into our world. We would be living in a different world.

Instead, look at the reality TV industry. *Keeping up with the Kardashians*? Here is a show about a family of people in LA, who don't seem to have jobs, and sit around talking about each other behind their backs. *Hoarders*? A camera crew invades the home of someone with a mental illness and exploits them. *Real Housewives*? Some women in my town were solicited by the producer of *Real Housewives* and asked if they would like to interview for *Real Housewives of Boston*. When the interviewer realized there wasn't any dirt, conflict, scandal, backstabbing or cheating going on amongst them, they were told, "Sorry, but you are too boring."

My point is this: somewhere along the line, our culture has veered away from the importance of love. As the rabbi asks, how can we stretch love, reach others with it, and try to understand each other better? The Dalai Lama echoes, "Love and compassion are necessities, not luxuries. Without them, humanity cannot survive...This is my simple religion...the philosophy is kindness."

Compassion is love. The Dalai Lama also proclaims, "In the Buddhist tradition, compassion and love are seen as two aspects of the same thing: Compassion is the wish for another being to be free from suffering; love is wanting them to have happiness." Research has shown that when we feel compassion, physiologic changes occur in our bodies. Our cardiovascular and nervous systems are affected, and we secrete oxytocin (the hormone released right after the birth of a baby that encourages bonding between mother and child). Because of these changes, certain regions of the brain associated with empathy, caregiving, and pleasure are activated, which often results in our wanting to approach and care for other people.

Giving. Giving to others, for the sake of the highest good of all concerned, keeps the heart energy circulating and helps us to attract the joy, or the healing, love and abundance that is out there waiting for us. Giving inspires the Law of Vibration, since giving feels good. When we give to others, either in service or financially, we are sending a message to the Universe that says, "I have enough and I want to share." Giving increases

our self-esteem (third chakra) and can transport us from a place of self-pity or sadness to placing our focus on others. Nothing lifts us up more than serving another person (or group of people, animals, plants, or the Earth) in need.

Imagine a group or cause that you would like to support, either with your time (service) or your money. Can you picture a child getting much-needed food, clothing, or school supplies? Can you see people at a food pantry getting food for their families? Can you see the bank checks filled with love and flying out around the community or the world? Imagine little hearts flying out of the envelopes as they go. (OK, that's my cheesy image; you don't have to use that one.) Create a picture in your mind of something or someone who, in receiving help and love (or money) from you, is affected in a positive way.

A note about creating more abundance with the heart chakra. One of the attractions of having more financial prosperity is a greater freedom to give to others financially. The more money we have in our lives, the more money we are able to share. Edwene Gaines, in *The Four Spiritual Laws of Prosperity*, says the most important way to increase abundance in our life is to tithe. Gaines recommends that you share at least ten percent of your income with others, regardless of how little money you may have. This concept goes back to the Law of Vibration: When you create within yourself a culture of giving, the vibration of freedom and abundance will tend to attract to you things that vibrate with that same frequency. That, in itself, is not the reason we should want to give. But there is a lesson here – the cosmic reward for generosity is the open, expansive, and happy feeling it creates. And although the prospect of financial gain is not a good reason to give to others, wanting to generate that wonderful feeling within yourself is a fine reason to give. The reward is setting up a different, open, abundant vibration that can actually change you.

Think of someone in your life who you would like to forgive or from whom you would like forgiveness. Imagine them smiling at you lovingly. Imagine that you are laughing together. (If this is a painful subject, don't pursue it. Sometimes the negative vibration overtakes the positive and winds up being too complicated for this meditation.)

It is the same idea for love, joy, or any other feeling you wish to attract into your life. I have always taught my children, "Output = input." You want me to be nicer to you? Start by being nicer to me! And so it goes.

Forgiveness. Forgiveness is essential for heart health. I am talking about the literal health of the organ. You can take co-enzyme Q10 and fish oil, eat your oatmeal, and run on a treadmill every day, but if you still have an unresolved issue with forgiveness, your heart will never be healthy.

As humans, we want to love and feel loved. When we are hurt by someone, it takes an act of courage to look deep inside our hearts and find love for that person. This concept is the meaning of forgiveness. The inability to forgive is the source of much havoc in our physical bodies. Whether it is the inability to forgive someone else or the need to be forgiven ourselves, this unresolved tension can eat us up. Often it is our need to forgive ourselves that proves to be the biggest task.

Ultimately, as hackneyed as it sounds, forgiveness is a gift to ourselves. When we are angry or resentful of another person, we unwittingly bind ourselves to that person, and that binding wastes a lot of our precious energy. Forgiveness means letting go of the ties that bind and releasing that negative energy. As we are willing and able to forgive people in our life, we will have more energy freed up to allow more good things into our life: joy, freedom, abundance, and love.

Perseverating thoughts and negative feelings about someone else are cumbersome weights to carry around with you each day, every day. Writer Anne Lamott explains, "I heard someone say that harboring resentment is like drinking rat poison and waiting for the rat to die. ...so therefore you are choosing to be toxic for the rest of your life, rather than to work and pray for the healing." Refusing to forgive will negatively affect your vibration keeping your energy in the place of resentment.

Do all three at once: love, serve, forgive. Picture a loved one and feel the profound buzz in the middle of your chest. Then, imagine the energy becoming an umbrella that reaches outward, infinitely, and engulfs all of the people who need help and those that you would like to forgive. Imagine love sheltering over all of it. Imagine enveloping the whole world with your vibration of love. What the world needs now is love, sweet love.

Forgiveness is perhaps our hardest work as humans. And like so many other things in life, it is like a muscle – it gets easier with practice. We are always being called to practice forgiveness with people who do unfathomable actions. I can only look back to the words of Rabbi Darby Leigh and attempt to reach for love, practice love, stretching it and sending it around the world to try to make a better place for all of us.

Workbook Questions and Ideas for the Fourth Chakra.

Answer the questions that are relative to you. You can answer as many or as few questions as you want. The goal is to isolate an easy and accessible image for the fourth chakra visualization. Remember, you can change your image any time you wish. You can also use these suggestions as a template for other questions.

Who do you love the most?

Who loves you the most?

What does love feel like to you? How does thinking of the people you love/who love you make you feel?

What are some organizations or causes that are most important to you?

What makes them important to you?

Who will benefit from your help, whether with time, service or monetary donation?

What issues motivate you to want to give? The environment? Religion or spirituality? Medical research? Poverty? Politics?

Whose forgiveness would you like?* Who needs your forgiveness? What would it feel like to be free of that negative tie that binds you to that person?

What would it feel like to forgive yourself?

**Forgiveness is tricky. Only write about forgiveness if the work feels productive. If thinking about someone who needs your forgiveness is painful or triggering, skip it in this meditation.*

Uplifting Ideas

Suggestions for the fourth chakra image.

When you are creating your fourth chakra image, choose pictures that incite love; a fullness and openness of the heart.

Here are some suggestions for uplifting ideas for your fourth chakra Elevate image:

- Someone you love deeply
- Someone who loves you deeply
- Giving to others in need
- Forgiving others (or yourself)
- The love umbrella: loving, giving and forgiving all at once under the same umbrella, which expands outward, filling the entire world

Because there are three separate gifts of the heart chakra, you can choose three different images, pick only one or two, or combine them all. The heart is such a powerful force; it dictates how we vibrate much of the time. Spending a little more time on this part of the meditation makes sense.

Whether you are using one of these uplifting images, or coming up with an idea of your own, choose an image that you can conjure quickly. Write a brief description of the image you have selected.

THE VOICE & THE WILL

Chakra 5

The Voice. The fifth chakra is located in the throat. One gift of the throat chakra is communication, or literally using your voice. The voice is how you communicate your truth to others, whether it's in relationships, school, work or out into the wider world. Are you communicating by using your full voice? Can you sing? Shout? Yell? Chant? Are you being heard?

Most Americans put public speaking at the top of their fear list. It is estimated that up to 74% of Americans have "glossophobia." Public speaking requires the activation of several chakras: acceptance from first chakra, creativity (what are you going to talk about?) from the second, self-esteem from the third. And it all comes from your "voice". What story do you have to tell? What is your truth? And how do you communicate to others?

Your voice is your voice – whether uttered out loud or written on the page. Any time you are expressing yourself, your feelings, your point of view, you are making yourself heard. It can be challenging, whether you are speaking or writing – it can leave you vulnerable and takes courage.

Women, men and the fifth chakra. In American culture, there are many systems that silence various groups of people because of race, gender, religious affiliation, or sexual preference. For women, it can be challenging to use our voices to express ourselves. It is not uncommon for a woman to be in a relationship in which she does not feel heard, in a job for which she does not feel adequately compensated, or in a role in which she does not feel respected.

Even a woman in a healthy relationship or business can feel hesitant to say what

Imagine writing a letter to someone with whom you would like to communicate. Imagine that person receiving that letter and understanding you in a deeper way..

she wants because of the stigma put on the "bitchy" or "high maintenance" woman. Recently, there was an article in the New York Times about what is currently known as "Resting Bitch Face" or RBF, the mistakenly-taken-for-unhappy accidental face a woman wears when caught off-guard in a photo. Are women allowed to non-verbally communicate only with smiles and sunshine? Do we all have to be perfect? There is now an app you can download that acts like a spell-checker, but instead of misspelled words, it highlights words that women often use in communication that convey a sense of inadequacy, inferiority, and doubt while diminishing confidence. These are words like, "just", "sorry", "I feel", and "does this make sense?" The problem seems to be ingrained in our DNA. The good news is that now, in the twenty-first century, we seem ready to start to change.

Imagine yourself speaking on a stage to a rapt audience. Imagine the audience giving you a raucous applause or a standing ovation. Imagine people laughing hard at your jokes, being moved by your performance, or provoked by your artwork. Feel your own rush of excitement, pride, and delight around making a difference in someone else's life because of something you said, sang, acted, or expressed yourself.

It is not just women who may have trouble communicating. Men can have just as much difficulty communicating as women, but often for different reasons and in different ways. Many people have trouble communicating their emotions. Relationships are difficult to maintain. Anyone who is married will tell you even the most loving of marriages take hard work – and the work is communicating. Being willing to truly express what you feel and what you believe – even if it is bound to make waves, is important in the work of a relationship. Even more important is to be able to tell others what you need. Sometimes you need help. Sometimes you don't want help. Sometimes you need more attention, to have someone reach out and touch your hand once in awhile. Sometimes what you need is to

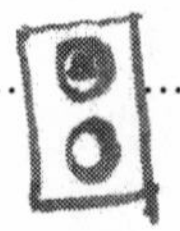

Imagine finishing a book you have been writing for years (ahem). Imagine the cover, what it looks like, how it feels to hold it in your hand. See people in a bookstore picking it up, buying it and reading it.

be left alone. Sometimes what you need is to be able to tell someone what you need.

Again, we see energy centers overlap. Declaring what you need is just as much a part of how worthy you feel (third chakra) and how much love you feel for (or from) the person with whom you are trying to communicate (fourth chakra). It can also have to do with tribal values that may or may not jibe with what you have to say (first chakra), let alone the power struggle inherent in many relationships (second chakra). Get it? This is not a gender-specific phenomenon, in work or in love. This is communication – the whole enchilada.

The will. The other gift of the fifth chakra is the will. Our will gives us the ability to make decisions and stick to them, to create discipline in our lives, to express our beliefs and stand firm in our reasons for those beliefs. The will is one of our intellectual faculties. It is another muscle that needs to be exercised. We exercise our will by developing discipline – rituals that we do each day or each week – and sticking to them. When we work this muscle more, we find that discipline comes easier. When we don't use it, we lose it; the will muscle atrophies, and we find ourselves having less direction and less focus.

In our culture today, when immediate gratification and mindless and unproductive entertainment are a literal finger tap away, it can be a huge challenge to exercise our will. Why would I want to write in my journal for an hour before I fall asleep when I can watch an episode of *Breaking Bad* on my iPad, which is right next to my bed? Or buy a pair of discount shoes on the web? Or catch up on Facebook? This is hard stuff. It takes work to overcome that obnoxious voice in our head that impedes our ability to stay focused, stay on task, and work the will.

Imagine a difficult conversation (which you have put off having) leading to a positive outcome. Imagine the person you are talking to ending your conversation with a smile and a hug.

The writer/humorist Mike Birbiglia refers to his obnoxious voice as "Sleepy Carl." Sleepy Carl is Mike's alter-ego who appears to him when he wakes up in the morning and convinces him that his need for more sleep far outweighs his need to wake up and be productive. Sleepy Carls are incredibly powerful and often dominate our inner debate of whether to sleep in or get up and at 'em! There are also big liars. (My inner obnoxious voice, of course, is named Sleepy Carol.)

When my children were little, sleep was a rare luxury in our house. The kids did not sleep through the night for years, and therefore, neither did the parents. One night, with exhaustion insomnia (parents of young children know what I'm describing – you are too tired to stay awake and too wired to fall back to sleep), I decided to go downstairs and turn on the TV. I don't usually do that, but it seemed like a good idea at the time. The TV was set on PBS, as it often was in those days (Elmo rules!) What I inadvertently turned on was a PBS fundraising telethon that featured Dr. Wayne Dyer doing his presentation, *Inspiration*. Wayne Dyer was an insightful psychologist who had a commanding presence and a powerfully deep, clear and compelling voice. At the very moment I turned on the TV, he was launching into his directive for how we can all have more success, productivity and happiness. "WAKE UP!" he said. "JUST WAKE UP!" He meant that literally.

If we could get ourselves to wake up earlier, we could seize the potential of this whole other part of the day, the morning, where things flow, ideas come, inspiration happens. "WAKE UP!" he yelled at the audience. Set your alarm, put your foot out of your bed, and slam it on the floor. Make yourself get up!

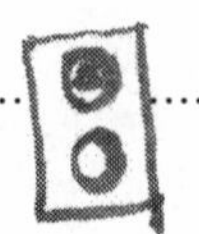

See yourself at the end of a daily practice. You just came back from your daily run with your face flushed. You just finished your meditation/ Elevate/yoga practice and are feeling a sense of calm.

It was certainly no coincidence that I stumbled upon those words. I decided to try it. Turns out it was incredibly helpful. Especially for a busy working parent – although sleep can be a problem if you don't have enough of it – waking thirty minutes earlier and having that extra time to read, write, think, or meditate helped me be a better, more patient parent, spouse, and worker for the rest of the day.

Dolly Parton, award-winning songwriter and performer, says, "I wake up early in the morning to do my dreaming....In the wee hours, the world is quiet and I can really listen to God." Waking early is also the mantra for many writers, poets, and artists. Mary Oliver, world-renowned poet, has a book of poetry titled, *Why I Wake Early*.

And yet, Sleepy Carl and Sleepy Carol are very good at their jobs. This is because of our under-utilized, under-exercised will muscles. Training the will is like weight training. It must be done with consistency and purpose. Sometimes it helps to understand that improving the strength of the will can lead to greater success and joy. Sometimes it doesn't help. Sometimes it is OK to falter now and again; after all, sleeping in can be a wonderful thing.

Where the will and the voice intersect In his audio book, *Meditations for Manifestation*, Wayne Dyer (here he is again) uses both the voice and the will to bring about change. *Meditations for Manifestation* utilizes the vocalization of the syllable "Aaaaaah" to help make desires and goals come to realization much faster.

I have done this meditation many times, and I have seen a few miracles as a result. As I mentioned before, in 2006, my husband and I and our two young children lived in a cute little house – I'd call it more like a cottage

– in a suburb of Boston. Our kids were growing up fast and we wanted more space. I was dissatisfied with several aspects of my house, including the fact that it sat very close to the Interstate and I could hear cars rushing past all day and all night, which drove me a little batty.

I sat down and made a list of things I really wanted in a new house. Since it was just a list, I let myself dream big. The list included a very light, window-filled room where I could put a grand piano (which I did not have at the time) and I could look out on a beautiful natural view while I played music. The list also included a large Jacuzzi tub, a screened-in porch, a finished basement room for the kids to play, and a fireplace.

The first action I took was to create a vision board using cutouts of pictures from home magazines, *Oprah* magazine, yoga retreat catalogues, and other sources of inspirational words.

I made Dr. Dyer's meditation into a daily ritual. I used my throat chakra to sound the syllable "Aaaaaah" and let it vibrate down my entire spine, down to the root and all the way back up to the top of my head. I had a vision of this windowed room and the view out of it. I saw all the different aspects of it. I saw it in every light and in every season and saw myself sitting near the windows playing Billy Joel or Bach on my grand piano (which I did not yet have). More importantly, I felt the feeling in my body of what it would be like when I was actually sitting in that room. I felt happiness and joy tingle around from my arms to my legs, all the while repeating the syllable "Aaaaaah." I cannot tell you how silly I felt doing it.

Very soon after (six to eight weeks later) a mutual friend told us about a house for-sale-by-owner in his neighborhood. In the back of the house was the living room, which had extra large windows on three sides, a perfect place for our grand piano (which we still did not have), and the view out to the meadow and 170 acres of conservation land behind it. It had all of my other requirements and, magically, was in our price range. The conservation land abutting the property had been in my husband's "Aaaaah" meditation. I knew in an instant it was my house.

Shortly after we moved into the house, a friend called to ask me if I had room for a grand piano. Her friend, a concert pianist, had been storing one of her prized baby grands at a storage facility and had recently found that it was getting damaged by the dust and humidity. She was looking for someone who would house the piano for her, who would love the piano and use it. Bingo! The piano came to me in a wildly unexpected way and fit perfectly in the place where I had been visualizing it for years.

Strengthening the will muscle does not mean you have to make a drastic change in your life. Nor does it mean you must institute the "hour of power" each morning, like all of the high-falutin' success gurus tell you. (Show me the person who can really do a full workout, then meditate and then journal a list of her intentions for the day in only one hour. I'd like to meet her.) It can simply mean putting a short discipline in place as a reminder, a place-holder, for being in the moment and allowing some goodness into your life for that moment.

Of course, not every meditation with the right mindset will bring about everything you wish for in your life. Life is still life, with its ups and downs and turnarounds. But Elevating your vibration to one of greater positivity allows for more good feelings to squeeze in there amidst the waves.

Workbook Questions and Ideas for the Fifth Chakra.

Answer the questions that are relative to you. You can answer as many or as few questions as you want. The goal is to isolate an easy and accessible image for the fifth chakra visualization. Remember, you can change your image any time you wish. Or you can use these suggestions as a template for other questions.

Some communication questions:

What kind of communicator are you?

Are there ways in which you communicate well with others? What is the emotion that comes with being understood by another person? What does it feel like to truly be seen or heard?

Do you have the desire to perform/speak/dance/sing/read in public?

Have you ever gotten your needs met because of words you said or wrote?

Some questions about the will:

In what ways are you disciplined in your life? In what ways could your discipline be improved?

Do you have daily practices or rituals? If yes, describe them.

What daily practices would you like to incorporate into your life?

How might your life be different if you did?

Note: Daily practice will mean different things to different people. For instance, you could do a fifteen minute yoga flow, a five minute gratitude rant, a one hour exercise regimen – the possibilities are endless. Elevate is a five or ten minute meditation. Can you imagine making that a daily ritual?

Uplifting Ideas

Suggestions for the fifth chakra image:

When you are creating your fifth chakra image, choose a picture that makes you feel excited, hopeful, or joyful around communicating with others. Visualize sustaining a discipline or practice.

Here are some suggestions for uplifting ideas for your fifth chakra Elevate image:

- Speaking in front of an audience
- Finishing a novel, a work of nonfiction, an article or a blog
- Writing a letter to communicate with someone
- Having a good outcome to a difficult conversation
- Having a successful daily practice: meditation, yoga, running, exercising

Because there are two separate gifts of the fifth chakra, you can choose one image, two different images or combine them. Whether you are using one of these uplifting images, or coming up with an idea of your own, choose an image that you can conjure quickly. Write a brief description of the image you have selected.

THE INTUITION, THE INTELLECT & WISDOM

Chakra 6

The sixth chakra is the third eye. This is where intuition resides. This is also where we form our beliefs, attitudes, and judgments. The sixth chakra is where we know truth and where we pay attention.

Intuition. Intuition is the ability to understand something immediately without the need for conscious reasoning. It is our "sixth sense," our sense of "knowing." In fact, I prefer the word "knowing," as it implies more of a subconscious action, an immediate sense of something, rather than the intellectual faculty of intuition.

A sixth chakra story. As a child, I had a very strong connection with my father. He was an unusual man – definitely on the wackier side. He was spiritual, open-minded, and believed very much in intuitive power. I have always been sensitive to energy, even as a little child. Sometimes, when I was very young, my dad would stare at the space between my eyebrows – my third eye – and it would start to tingle. It was actually a little annoying when my dad would do this. He was doing it to be playful (this was his sense of humor) and to show how connected we were. But it was also really weird. None of the other dads did that. When my parents split up and my dad moved out, I found that I didn't need to be with him for it to happen. I would be sitting in my bedroom, and my third eye would start to tingle. I'd call my dad and say, "Could you please stop that?" He would reply, "I was calling. Glad you heard me." I would roll my eyes. My dad passed away in 2002. Sometimes I randomly feel my third eye tingle, and it gives me the willies.

I have had several experiences with my intuition that have sent chills up my spine. They have only happened a handful of times, and it's not something I work at. "Knowing" is different. Knowing is something I use in my work every day. As a healer, I have to "know" what someone needs from me in the moment, and this ability is another use of my intuition. That part of my intuitive muscle gets used constantly. Sometimes, out of nowhere, I get the idea to ask a patient a weird question, such as, "Did someone in your life pass away recently? Are you angry at yourself for something? Do you have a toothache?" When it first started happening, it

took a major leap of faith for me to actually tell the patient about what I was hearing. I didn't want to be seen as weird or creepy. Again, we work our muscles, and now when I get the compulsion to ask the question that has "randomly" popped into my head, it often turns out to be pretty accurate. The weirdest one was the time I asked a patient if she had eaten something strange. My intuitive sense was picking up something being off in her stomach, and the question just came to me. This is not a question I generally ask, but I asked it anyway. Her eyes got very wide, and she said, "Yesterday I ate a giant clam." Woop woop.

Intellectual faculties. We can know a lot about our environment by using our five senses: sight, touch, hearing, smell, and taste. Animals also have those five senses. Our senses allow us to survive in our environment. However, it is our intellectual faculties that make us higher level thinkers, dreamers and relators – and that is what separates us from the animals. These are faculties like reasoning, perspective, imagination, and memory. Again, like our muscles, if the faculties don't get used, they shrink and wither; they atrophy. And like muscles, when they do get used, they grow and expand.

Imagination. Imagination is one of those right-brained concepts that is free-flowing, creative, and non-linear. If you are an accountant and spend your days looking at lines of numbers and figuring out complex numerical relationships, you may not have much time or inclination to make art. So if someone asks you to paint a watercolor, make up a children's story, or write a song, you might be lost. But if you set aside a few minutes every day to write, paint, or do something imaginative, this creative process will come to you more easily. This is why so many writers talk about getting up every day and writing, even if they have nothing to say. It is a mental, creative work-out.

Perspective. Perspective is also a muscle. Perceiving something from another person's viewpoint is something that must be practiced. It is part of the practice of compassion, non-judgment, and love.

I heard a story on the *Moth Radio Hour* on NPR that was told by Karen Jones, the author of the blog, *See Our Soldier, A Chronicle of Healing*. Her story is about the heartbreak of growing up with an alcoholic father who never took interest in her life. The setting was the sixties, when she was a teenager. She had asked her dad to come see her play in a powder-puff football game. He declined, as he always did. She asked again and again – each time he said "No." On game day, she looked up and saw that her dad was in the stands. She was elated and started out the game playing her best. At half-time, it started to snow and she saw him walk out of the stands and leave the field. She was deflated with disappointment. When she returned home, he was drunk and passed out on the couch.

When her father passed away years later, she had trouble writing a eulogy. She couldn't find words to express anything positive about him. Doing research with her brother about his life, she found out that her father had fought in The Battle of the Bulge of WWII. They Googled "Battle of the Bulge" and spent time reading about the 1.1 million soldiers who fought and the unspeakable atrocities they saw. Thousands died from the awful conditions, especially horrendous during the winter when the soldiers had to sleep on the ground covered in snow. She learned how it was the largest and bloodiest battle of World War II and ultimately the one that led to the demise of Germany. She realized for the first time that her dad was a hero among heroes, even though he hadn't asked to be. She thought about the intensity of the noise of the fighting, the crowds, the cold. She realized that her father must have had profound PTSD and had quietly suffered with his memories. Because of her new perspective, she now was able to see that coming to her football game, with the noise, the crowds and in the cold and snow, was a profound act of love and courage. Perspective changes everything.

Perspective 2.0. When I was in chiropractic college, I took a class on addiction. I learned to recognize the signs of addiction and learned the term ACoA, or Adult Child of an Alcoholic. There was a list of signs and symptoms of ACoA, and as I went down the list, I realized I had most of

Spend a day NOT judging. If you catch yourself judging someone else, apologize to them in your head. Notice how you feel at the end of the day.

them. This was shocking, as neither of my parents were alcoholics. But as I thought about it and started to ask questions, I realized that my father was an addict. The phrase 'sex addict' hadn't been coined in popular culture yet, so I wasn't quite sure it was a "thing," but my father was a 'womanizer'. Once my parents' marriage ended, people excused his inappropriate behavior as "mid-life crisis". My brother and I chuckled uncomfortably when he gave his number to the waitress at every restaurant. At family events, holidays, Bar Mitzvahs or weddings, he had a different woman standing with him in the table picture. It turned out that my father's problem was not a silly preoccupation with girls; it was a serious addiction. The subject was sex, but it could have easily been something else.

As a young adult, I had become thoroughly disgusted with my dad's past lascivious behaviors. I felt he had put his own interests way before mine (which was true) and had put me in awkward positions to have to lie to my mother constantly (which was also true). And as a young feminist, his actions were anathema to who I was and how I felt about love and relationships. However, my discovery of his addiction was helpful to me. Seeing my dad as an addict gave him more humanity in my eyes. Seeing his actions as a pathology and giving them the name of "addiction" gave me a totally different perspective. My father must have had to battle some big demons in his life, and he lost those battles much of the time. I know that people do the best they can, and sometimes the best they can do is limited by other factors, such as a big fat addiction sitting on their shoulder. The forgiveness has not come easily. But with the diagnosis, came a reason for compassion. And that was a start.

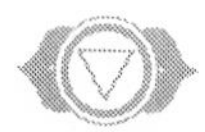

Judgment. In 2004, one of my mentors assigned me the "Love Everyone" exercise. The rules are simple. For one whole week (seven full days) you must love everyone with whom you come into contact no matter what. If you have a negative, mean, or judgmental thought about someone, you start the week again at day one. This exercise is way harder than it sounds. It took a few days for me to get used to loving everyone no matter what, which, as you can imagine, made the exercise much longer than one week. Sad but true.

"Love Everyone" may sound like a heart chakra exercise, because of the love piece. But it's actually a sixth chakra exercise because of the judgment piece. I learned a great deal about myself that week. I noticed that, over the years, I had become something along the lines of a judgmental b____! Becoming aware of how much I judged others was shocking.

The satirical newspaper *The Onion* once ran a headline that read "Woman In Coffee Shop Judges A Record 147 People." The article describes how one woman "broke her own record for judgmental behavior when she judged 147 fellow customers, passersby, and motorists in an almost constant stream of criticism during the 25 minutes it took her to enjoy a soy-mocha frappachesso at Portland's Eagle's Roast Monday." Life imitating art.

Because of the Law of Attraction (that I will talk about in a later chapter), when we judge others, we ourselves feel judged. During my week of loving everyone, I was able to examine how many assumptions I made about people. To see someone, for example, put out a cigarette butt on the street – an act which, ordinarily, would inflame me – and be obligated to feel love for that person was hard work. I had to let go of the assumption that the person had no love for the environment. I had to let go of the assumption that the person did not care about his health. I had to stop myself from judging the person as a total asshole, just because he threw a cigarette butt on the ground.

Try to recognize that everyone is good at something. Maybe the guy throwing his trash out of the car window on the highway is a really talented guitar player. Maybe the woman yelling at her son on the bus serves the homeless at a soup kitchen on the weekends. Maybe the kid who bullied my daughter in first grade will grow up to be a really good painter. Imagining the best in someone is a practice to raise your own vibration.

Instead, I had to say to myself, "I don't know if that person is having a bad day, if his wife left him this morning, if he struggles with depression or insomnia or addiction. I don't know anything about that person." I had to find the compassion for a person who does not know that it is better for the environment to put out a cigarette and throw it in the trash than to throw it on the sidewalk. Maybe that person is an environmentalist and runs ten miles a day, but got some really bad news and was compelled to smoke a cigarette for the first time since he quit twenty years ago. Maybe there were no trashcans in sight, and he was in a rush.

The exercise was life-changing. At the end of the week of loving everyone, I felt like a different person. I was seeing colors brighter and seeing a little more sparkle in everything. I was more loving, patient, accepting and – in a word – happier. That week, I realized a new truth; We are all much more the same than we are different. When we take the time to imagine walking in someone else's shoes, expend the energy to NOT judge, and examine all of the assumptions we make about others, we win.

Soon after the week of loving everyone, I walked by my receptionist's desk and saw that the screen-saver she had chosen for her computer read "The beloved in disguise just walked through the front door." Exactly.

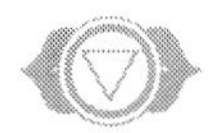

Because it made me feel so good, I tried to incorporate the "love-everyone" exercise into my life and practice. That lasted for about two hours. The exercise is too hard to be sustainable. So I found a way to make it more true for myself. Instead of "loving everyone", I chose "respecting something about everyone".

Think of something that represents truth to you: a spiritual practice, a particular book, a philosophy, a movement, a jury, or a panel of judges.

Like forgiveness, letting go of judging others will change your life, set you free, and allow you to receive more gifts from your own life.

Wisdom. Wisdom, in human terms, combines experience, knowledge, perspective, and good judgment. Good news: Wisdom increases with age. My friends in their fifties, sixties, and beyond have this one thought in common. Despite all of the increasing aches and pains and other hard things that come with age, the gift is wisdom. With the advancing years comes a new wisdom that guides us, calms us, and elevates us. In my better moments, I am eagerly welcoming the wisdom of age. It is a nice contrast to worrying about my neck getting saggy.

For me, the ultimate wisdom resides in nature. It always thrills me to walk deep into the woods and appreciate that I am an onlooker. A very complex ecosystem exists and has existed for millennia without me. When I lived in Portland, Oregon, I fell in love with a small rustic retreat center in the mountains called Breitenbush Hot Springs. At Breitenbush, there is a small wooden bridge that crosses over a gently rushing river. I have spent many hours on that bridge throughout my life. I stand against the rail, watching the water as it flows toward me and then I turn around and lean against the opposite rail and watch the water as it flows away. The water never stops coming and never stops going. We can't keep the water; we have to let it go. It is the ultimate intellect, intuition, and wisdom of the Universe. It is inevitable that the water is going to come down from the mountain, travel under your bridge, keep on flowing, and disappear

Picture yourself at eighty, ninety, or one hundred years old, still vibrant and active with gray hair and a calm smile (or dyed blond hair, or no hair!). Picture yourself sharing your wise words with another person who wants to learn from you.

around the bend.

Wisdom about change. Change is constant; nothing remains the same. In her book, *Anatomy of the Spirit*, Carolyn Myss states, "Mentally we can absorb that [change is constant] with little difficulty. Yet when change occurs in our lives, when we notice we are aging, when people we love die, or when relationships shift from being intimate and loving to distant – this truth terrorizes us." Yet, this is life. Life is change. Life is the river flowing toward us, under the bridge, and then away from us forever.

Attention. The biggest lesson I have learned from my rapidly-growing wisdom is the importance of paying attention. When my dear friend Ronna was diagnosed with terminal cancer, she downloaded an app onto her phone called Headspace. The creator of Headspace is Andy Puddicombe,* an English former-monk trained in Tibetan Buddhism. His mission, after returning home from travels all over Asia, was to make "meditation and mindfulness accessible, relevant and beneficial to as many people as possible." With the app one can create a practice – a ten, fifteen, or twenty minute meditation either with Andy's voice and direction or with silent, unguided time. It's a simple tool with a simple message. The benefits of sitting in stillness and paying attention go beyond just quieting the mind.

Andy Puddicombe info from Wikipedia: "Do Lectures." Retrieved 19 March 2014.

What represents wisdom to you? Is it a person? A teacher? An old oak tree? A star? Or is it something man-made, like a great book or work of art? Is it a productive meeting or discussion that brings together the intellect with the intuition?

For Ronna, newly diagnosed with a terminal illness and not particularly interested in talking about it, this was her anchor. Sitting in meditation with Andy each day was her respite from her anxiety and the dark places. When I visited her, we would sit together, listening to Andy in silence, breathing, and just being. Those are precious memories for me, the gift of paying attention together. I haven't been able to listen to Andy since she passed, as his voice reminds me that she is gone. I know that at some point, hearing his lovely baritone English-accented voice will bring me comfort and bring me closer to Ronna again.

I was on vacation, staying with some cousins in California, when I got the news that Ronna had passed away. The next morning, before dawn, I was awakened by an urgent feeling. "Go outside," I heard. I rolled over. It was dark, and I did not know my way around the house, nor did I know if there was a place to sit outside. "Go outside," the voice declared. "Go!" In the dark, I begrudgingly got up and put on a sweatshirt. Still half-asleep, I walked to the back of the house and quietly opened the back door, praying there was no alarm set that would wake the house and neighborhood at 4:30 in the morning. I walked outside and saw a bench on the back deck facing the yard. I sat down on the bench, criss cross applesauce. Then I waited. I waited. I waited. What was I waiting for? Ronna, you told me to come out here. Aren't you going to present me with some miracle? Will there be a fabulous animal, like an elk, walking through the back yard, or a peacock with feathers plumed, to prove you are making contact with me from the afterlife? What is the deal, Ronna? Why did you get me up so early?

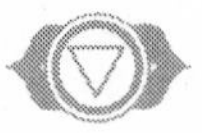

Picture a river flowing toward you, beneath you, or away from you. Picture a stand of old pine trees, knowing they are all connected underground by their roots, yet stand majestically tall as they have for ages.

There were lots of birds, and a sunrise, and I started to see the lovely flowers and trees in the backyard (those are miracles, mind you). Finally, it hit me. I realized what I was doing. I was on a bench, seated in a yoga-like position. I was meditating. She wanted me to meditate with her. I felt her there. There was no pomp and circumstance, there were no fireworks, there was no Andy. It was just me and her sitting, paying attention quietly, together.

Paying attention doesn't necessarily mean sitting in a formal meditation. It can just mean remembering to take a breath and feel the air going through your nose and out of your mouth. Feeling the air rising in your chest and receding again. Remembering to experience through your five senses. Taking a moment to ask, what am I seeing? What am I smelling? Is there a taste in my mouth? How does my butt feel on this chair? Is there any noise around me? Taking one moment to go through this little exercise can mean more than we realize. Jon Kabat-Zinn, Professor Emeritus at the University of Massachusetts Medical School, and creator of the Mindfulness Based Stress Reduction program, teaches that how you pay attention to your life can actually change your life, your biology, and your brain.

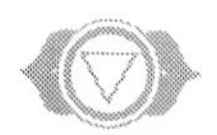

As the poets will tell you, paying attention helps you realize the miracles in life you take for granted. Even the rise and fall of your chest as you breathe is a miracle. Albert Einstein said, "There are only two ways to live your life. One is as though nothing is a miracle. The other is as though everything is a miracle." If you are lucky enough to remember to pay attention, and appreciate miracles throughout your day, that's your ticket to a very high vibration. This is the gift of Elevate. Elevate will remind you to be mindful and appreciative, and to pay attention, each and every day.

Picture being in the middle of a beautiful garden on a little stone bench, being quiet and paying attention. Picture being in the middle of a forest, no one around, and paying full attention. Picture sitting on the sand in front of a beautiful blue body of water, noticing warmth coming from the earth and radiating up into your body. What emotions do you feel?

Workbook Questions and Ideas for the Sixth Chakra.

Answer the questions that are relative to you. You can answer as many or as few questions as you want. The goal is to isolate an easy and accessible image for the sixth chakra visualization. Remember, you can change your image any time you wish. Or you can use these suggestions as a template for other questions.

Have you had experiences that made you feel intuitive? If so, what were they and what was it like to "know" something?

Do you feel more intuitive in a place of worship? In nature? In dreams?

Are you judgmental? What is something you feel judgmental about? What would it feel like to let go of that judgment and choose acceptance or understanding instead?

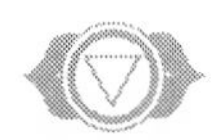

Do you feel judged by others? In what way?

How would it feel if you knew you were not being judged? What might you do differently without fear of being judged?

Do you find wisdom in the natural world: a river, a tall tree, the ocean, or the starry night?

Is there a particular book, song, movie, or poem that represents wisdom to you? Is there a person in your life who is very wise?

Do you practice mindfulness? If so, what emotion is attached to the practice? If not, what do you think it would feel like to be more mindful?

Can you think of an everyday miracle? A sunrise? A robust vegetable garden? An act of kindness? A smile from a stranger?

Uplifting Ideas

Suggestions for the sixth chakra image:

When you are creating your sixth chakra image, choose a picture that reminds you of truth,non-judgment, wisdom. Choose an image that reminds you to be mindful.

Here are some suggestions for uplifting ideas for your sixth chakra Elevate image:

- A time when you "knew" something
- Someone in your life who does not judge you
- Your favorite representation of truth or wisdom; a poem, a philosopher, a great leader whose words ring true
- Someone wise; imagine yourself as the wise one
- The wisdom of nature; a stand of old pine trees, a rushing river, the ocean tide, a mountain
- Paying attention in a forest, a garden, or some other place you love

Whether you are using one of these uplifting images, or coming up with an idea of your own, choose an image that you can conjure quickly. Write a brief description of the image you have selected.

THE CROWN

Chakra 7

Imagine that your relationship with the Universe is a friendship and needs time and attention to allow it to flourish and grow. Imagine that sitting with God is like sitting with an old friend with whom you do not need to chit chat, but merely to sit in each others' presence and feel love together.

Seventh chakra. The seventh chakra is our connection to Source, The Universe, The Something-Else-Out-There. It is located at the crown of the head, where our energy can connect with the Universal Energy. Some will call this God, but you don't have to believe in God to believe that there is a universal energy that organizes us, guides us, and keeps things moving along. The seventh chakra is the prayer chakra, our connection to the Divine and to the outer world. Through this chakra, we remember that we are connected to something bigger than ourselves: The Universal Energy that powers all living things.

Connecting with spiritual energy is an intensely personal experience. Spiritual influences in our childhood have great influence on how (or if) we will worship or appreciate the divine, but they don't always pan out like parents hope they will. My husband and I spent thousands of dollars on our children's Bar and Bat Mitzvah celebrations, but that did not ensure their connection to Judaism. In fact, I promised my daughter that, when she turned eighteen, she could (and should) walk her own path even if it was the path right out of our synagogue. She reminded me of that last Yom Kippur, when she turned to me with a wink and said, "This is my last time in this building!" Epic fail? Maybe, maybe not. We shall see what happens as she continues her journey into adulthood and hopefully becomes a parent herself.

First Buddha. When I was fourteen, my father was an exchange professor at the University of Bangkok in Thailand. I spent the summer of ninth grade in a lush, tropical, dirty, noisy, exotic, cosmopolitan city. And it was during monsoon season! Despite the daily one-hour avalanche of rain,

my dad planned many activities for us throughout the summer – trips to museums, shopping, sampling spicy noodles from pushcarts, and visiting Buddhist temples. Buddhist temples, called wats, are abundant in Thailand and are a big draw for tourists. They are magnificent structures with beauty and extravagance that can take your breath away. Each has a Buddha inside. There are jade Buddhas, golden Buddhas, marble Buddhas – you name it. It was quite a culture shock for this teenager. I spent most of the time glued to my Walkman headphones (Earth Wind and Fire, 1980!) and was mainly interested in sitting out at the pool before the monsoon and tanning in my teeny bikini. I was not remotely interested in wats.

Imagine that the crown of the head is the spot that Universal love can pour into you. The top of your head is a goblet that holds all the love, light, water, rays of sunlight, or color you can pour into it. And from the goblet, all of this seeps into your body, down into all of your cells. Use a yellow light, or green, or purple, or whatever color moves you.

My father was a JewBu. Although he was raised Jewish, as an adult he became interested in Buddhism (years before it was hip). My dad strived to weave spirituality into his complicated life. In the 1960's, he was active in the Humanistic Judaism movement, and wrote much of their liturgy: High Holiday services and our Passover Haggadah. He also learned to meditate (years before meditating was hip). For much of my childhood, my father wore a small amulet of the Buddha on a leather strap around his neck. He was the epitome of hip. Hip-itome.

Being in Thailand was a spiritual banquet for my dad. He loved going into the temples to have his *experience*. He would enthusiastically take off his shoes, light a candle, and take his seat on the floor. He would bow down to the Buddha and be off-line for varying periods of time.

Imagine yourself taking a shower. The water flows out of the shower head, down onto the crown of your head, and then down your neck, shoulders, arms, trunk, hips, legs, feet, and into the earth (via the drain) to start the cycle again. You can see this flow as water, gold, life-force, color, or dollar bills – whatever resonates the most.

It was a whole other issue having a fourteen year-old American teeny-bopper (as he affectionately referred to me) in tow. But with my father being my father, he would make me take off my shoes, hand me a candle, and insist I sit down on the mat next to him. I obliged him by taking off my shoes and holding the candle, but I would not bow. That was just going above and beyond my comfort level. I wanted to be at the pool. I was self-conscious. Wasn't it enough that I was sitting barefoot in someone else's house of worship inhaling smelly incense? No bowing, no way.

As the weeks went by there were more sightseeing trips and more wats. It was like going to Italy and viewing major works of art every day. They are beautiful and special, but after a time you get tired of them. After a few days on a boat in Alaska, I imagine one gets tired of seeing whales and icebergs. That was me with wats.

One weekend toward the end of the summer, we journeyed up to the city of Chiang Mai in the mountains of northern Thailand. On our first day in Chiang Mai, we climbed the 309 steps up to Wat Doi Sutep, the city's most famous temple. (These days, there is a tram that will take you up the 3500 feet elevation, but in 1980 it was old-school.) I had skipped up the 309 steps faster than anyone else and arrived at the temple alone. It was a cloudy day and the courtyard had a misty, ethereal feel. I wandered around by myself, feeling very out of breath and at the same time, finding the place breathtaking. I don't know what happened to the others in our party at that moment; it was like everyone else vanished, and I was alone at the top with all of the statues of the Buddha. It's hard for my fifty year-

old brain to remember exactly what happened to my fourteen year-old self, but there I was literally in a cloud, with my mind feeling at peace. I walked by a small out-building lined with statues. A stillness took over as I stopped in front of a small, plain, stone Buddha sitting all the way to the left of the others. Her face was quiet and peaceful, and she was wearing a half-smile. (I now recognize her as Quan Yin.) She was looking at me, looking through me. I dropped to my knees and began to cry. I had no idea why. I bowed before her. She was me, or God, or something I recognized deeply. This was my first time. I didn't realize it in the moment, but I had lost my spiritual virginity.

Imagine opening a window to easily slip into the connectedness of the Divine. Just push it open and feel the air rush in at you, be with you, and surround you with positive energy.

Spirituality has unfolded in my life since then, in many different contexts. In my twenties, I lived in Israel and got a bolder taste of Judaism and a sense of our rich and complicated history. For a while after that, I got into Native American spirituality. In my thirties, I looked into the eyes of my own children for the first time and found a connectedness I had not known before. I yearned for them to have a relationship with something bigger than themselves. So I leaned backward into Judaism (as many people do when they have kids) to provide them with a structure for spiritual seeking. That's how I became involved in a strong Jewish community. In my forties, I went even further, becoming a Bat Mitzvah at age forty-eight and joining the Board of my temple. Sometimes I buzz with connectedness, but those moments are not the norm of my day to day life. Most of the time I live my moments oblivious to the Divine around me. But like other things in life, a little practice goes a long way. I know that when I exercise that muscle of paying attention to the divine miracles in the everyday moments, it's easier to simply tap into the spirit of all things.

I remember you. As part of my personal Elevate process, when I get to the seventh chakra, I say out loud, "I remember you." I remember that there is a Universal Energy, God, Source, something bigger than me and I give thanks for the unconditional love, peace and guidance from which it emanates. Father James Martin, a well-known Jesuit priest and writer, says that we can see our relationship with the divine the way we see a precious friendship. There are friends with whom we can sit and say nothing and still feel their joyous presence and strong love connection. Yet as in any friendship, there is a certain amount of tending that is required in order for a friendship to last. We need to put time into our friendships, and energy, and love. The same is true for our relationship with God, says Father Martin. We need to devote time to sitting easily with God in order to nurture our relationship with the spiritual. This can be done anywhere; it does not need a special sanctuary or temple. For me, this takes off a lot of pressure. At any time, I can feel connected. At any time, I can turn around and hang out with God. How cool is that?

Gratitude. At the end of your Elevate meditation, sit for a few moments in gratitude. You can do a "Rampage of Appreciation" (from the *Teachings of Abraham*), where you make a list of everything you can think of for which you are grateful, or just pick one or two things that bring you joy, peace, ease, space. You can choose big things or little things. You can be grateful for a blue sky, or rain, or your breath or your breakfast. You can be grateful for having five minutes to sit and focus and Elevate. Simply put, gratitude is a fantastic closer, whether you are walking off into your day, walking off into the sunset, or drifting off to sleep.

Workbook Questions and Ideas for the Seventh Chakra:

Answer the questions that are relative to you. You can answer as many or as few questions as you want. The goal is to isolate an easy and accessible image for the seventh chakra visualization. Remember, you can change your image any time you wish – every day, if you like. You can use these suggestions as a template for other questions.

How do you imagine the Divine or Universal energy?

In your mind is it represented as a person? Is it the breathtaking canvas of a starry night? Or the breathtaking canvas of Van Gogh's *Starry Night*?

Is it a tall, snow-covered mountain? A stand of huge pine trees? The inner design of a brightly colored flower?

Is it a smiling presence? A buddha? A blooming flower garden?

Is it rays of sunlight coming out of the clouds?

What images come to mind when

you think of the interconnectedness of all life?

Do you see something from nature? Trees? Mountains? Animals? Insects?

Do you see people loving each other?

Can you imagine people of different races, ethnicities, or regions having DNA so similar there are only .00001% differences?

Have you ever experienced something in your life that could be described as "magic?"

What do you think about coincidences? Is there something or someone in your life that you would describe as coming from Divine connection or Divine intervention?

Uplifting Ideas

Suggestions for the seventh chakra image:

When you are creating your seventh chakra image, choose a picture that reminds you of your connection to the Universe, the divine, the Source of all.

Here are some suggestions for uplifting ideas for your seventh chakra Elevate image:

- Universal love (in the form of golden light) pouring into the top of your head and filling you from your feet up to the top of your head
- Taking a shower in divine light (instead of water)
- Sitting down in friendship with God, as one would sit and have tea with a good friend

Whether you are using one of these uplifting images, or coming up with an idea of your own, choose an image that you can conjure quickly. Write a brief description of the image you have selected.

Gratitude *When you finish your Elevate practice, take a minute to sit in gratitude. Here are some ideas for gratitude images:*

- *An important person in your life*
- *A beautiful morning sky*
- *You being in the present moment and meditating*

Breathe, be present, smile.

Elevate Cheat Sheet

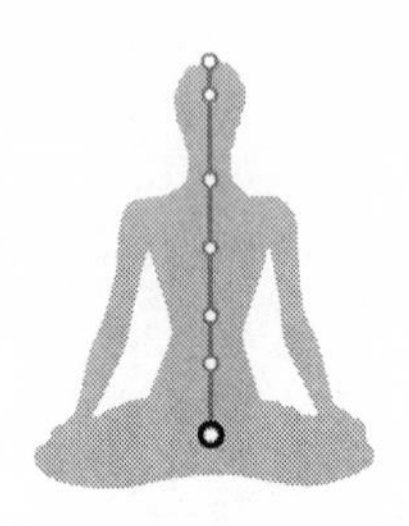

CHAKRA 1:

Location of buzz:
tailbone, bum, pelvic floor

Image: ______________________

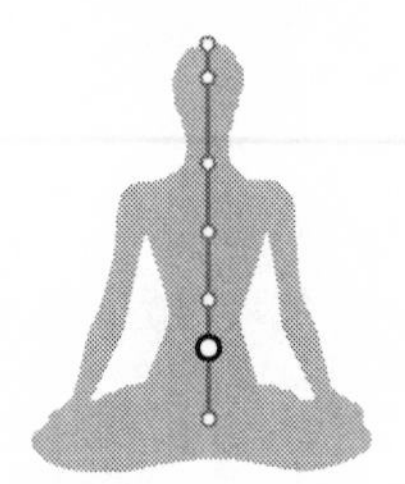

CHAKRA 2:

Location of buzz:
lower abdomen

Image: ______________________

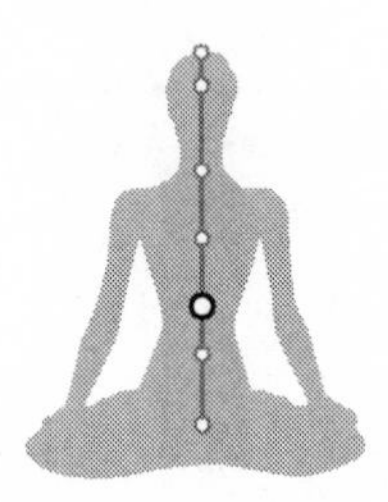

CHAKRA 3:

Location of buzz:
just under rib cage, belly, Dan Tian

Image: ______________________

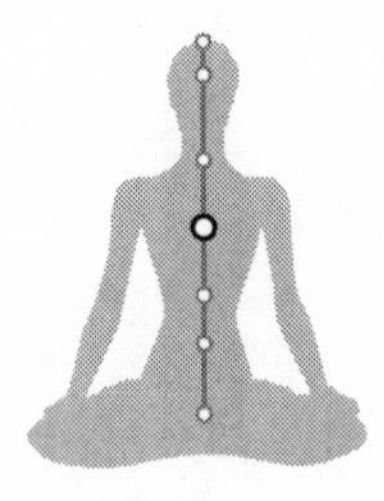

CHAKRA 4:

Location of buzz:
heart, chest

Image: ______________________

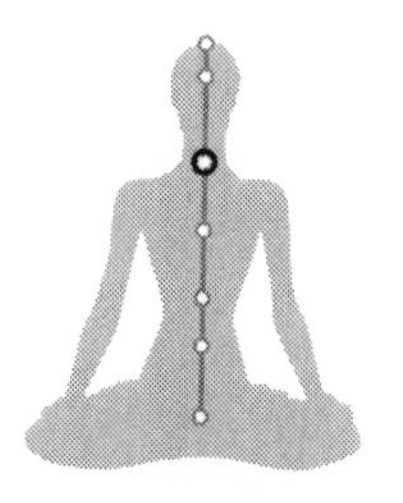

CHAKRA 5:

Location of buzz:
throat

Image:

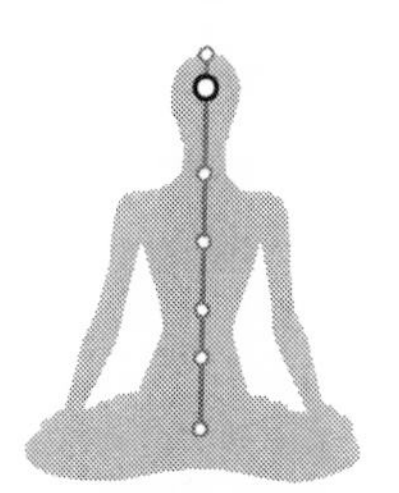

CHAKRA 6:

Location of buzz:
third eye, between the eyebrows

Image:

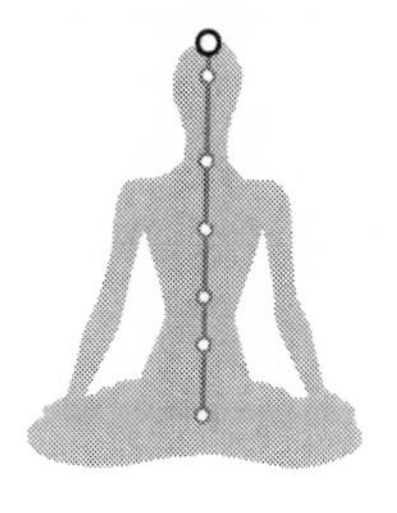

CHAKRA 7:

Location of buzz:
crown of the head

Image:

GRATITUDE:

Closer:
what you are grateful for

Image:

PART 3
THOUGHTS ABOUT LIFE THAT MIGHT HELP YOU ELEVATE

LAW OF ATTRACTION

The Law of Attraction says that we attract to us things that resonate with our own vibration. In other words, what you focus on in your life will draw in other things that have that same energy. If you tend to see life as one problem after another, or focus on what is not working in your life, you will attract more things that are problematic and negative into our life. When you focus more on the beauty of things, you will see more things of beauty come into your life.

I realize this may be too much of a simplification for many people. Life is life, and life delivers many different kinds of experiences to us as we live it. The Law of Attraction is indeed simple. If it makes you squirm, try to breathe through it and grasp some of its wisdom as, not the be-all-end-all of credos, but a tool to help live a more peaceful, happy life.

I first learned about the Law of Attraction from a book called *Ask and it is Given*, by Esther and Jerry Hicks. The book includes the "Teachings of Abraham," which are writings based on a collective spiritual entity that is channeled by Esther Hicks. Abraham imparts wise lessons about life and spirituality, health and wellness, love and forgiveness, all based on one thing: The Law of Attraction. For some, the idea of channeling spirits is too preposterous to give credence; Esther is immediately discarded as if she is a creepy, quacky kook. She herself jokes that she talks to dead people for a living.

I learned about Esther in 2005 at age 40. I was as open as ever to the magic and mystery of the world at that time. I loved what Abraham had to say and I embraced the teachings, impressed by the way the words inspired positive consciousness, ethical living, possibility-based thinking and gratitude. After reading *Ask and it is Given*, I felt that humans could do anything using the right amount of positivity and belief.

As I studied, I began to change the emphasis in my healing practice from talking about bones and muscles to talking more about the importance of positive attitudes and their effect on health. I started using the Law of

Attraction to build my practice, setting my intention to attract the ideal patients to me who would respond best to my care. I did Law of Attraction exercises to bring things into my life that I knew would make my life better.

The Teachings of Abraham were not, for me, about having more success or making more money. They were about learning how to create my own happiness. Through my studies, I was able to empower myself to go outside my comfort zone in order to experience growth and positive change. I was also on a mission to help others do the same.

In 2006, I began a study group with twelve women that met once a month. We explored the Law of Attraction together. One of the women in the group was working for corporate America and was miserable in her job. She had four children and a few grandchildren and found she barely had enough time for them, let alone for her true passion of gardening. She explained to the group that she absolutely could not leave her 9-to-5 job, as it provided health insurance for her family. Our meetings helped her see that she needed a vision for what she wanted to attract into her life, rather than a defensive excuse for why she was stuck. One evening, our group did an exercise of creating vision boards for our five-year future plan. While she was gluing pictures of flowers and plants on her board and thinking about how wonderful it would be to work with her hands in the earth every day, the idea for a company name popped into her head; "The Duchess of Dirt." A few years later, the Duchess opened her business – complete with its own health insurance – and today she has so much business she has a staff of many employees!

In an earlier chapter, I described making a vision board when I wanted to find a new house. I sat and meditated on what an upgrade would look like – remember I wanted the screened-in porch (for the mosquitoes), the fireplace, and the big bath tub? I also wanted big windows that looked out into woods. I wanted a farmhouse minus the farm. My husband and son wanted a place to play football in the back yard, so that went into the vision as well. But beyond the material elements of my ideal home, I had been longing for a greater sense of community which I hadn't found with our current home. For example, the first anniversary of 9/11 fell on the day of our annual neighborhood block party. The Boston area was hit hard by the tragedy and it felt important to me to mark the day with some sort of ritual, even while we were having our yearly neighborhood bash. My idea was to have everyone stand in a big circle, each of us holding a candle. We would light one candle and have each person light their candle off the next person until we were all standing together in a circle of light. I am a sucker for this kind of thing; community connection, togetherness, *Kumbaya*! Admittedly, I often get ridiculed about my tendency toward *Kumbaya* by various friends and family members. My neighbors followed suit. It turns out, not everyone loves *Kumbaya*. My neighbors obliged, as kind and lovely as they were, but I could tell that (with a few exceptions) people felt awkward and this circle-candle stuff was not their cup of tea.

So several years later, when I was making the vision board, I glued the word "COMMUNITY" right onto the middle. (Warning: Be careful what you wish for.) I hung the board on the wall of my bedroom so I could stare at it every day for a few minutes. Within about six weeks, we learned of a house available in a co-housing community. We had heard of co-housing, but we weren't sure exactly what it was or if it would be right for our family. Intrigued, we went and had a look at the house. It was a red farmhouse, with big windows in the living room that looked out on a meadow (perfect for football) and 170 acres of conservation land behind it. It had a large bath tub. It had a screened-in porch and a fireplace. It was in our price range. When I saw the house, the hair on my arms stood on end and I got chills down my spine. I knew.

A co-housing community is a cross between a condo complex and a commune. Neighbors own their own property, but many things are shared. Although we have our own homes, and mostly our own comings and goings, we do many things in community; make decisions together, landscape and garden together, celebrate lifecycle events, process world events, watch the Patriots, put on plays, have meals once a week. I have to laugh when I remember myself gluing the word "Community" onto the middle of the board. One cannot get more "community" than co-housing. *Kumbaya*!

The other word that I put on the board in big letters was, "CHANGE." I do not recommend this unless you have really thought it through! First, our lives got very crazy while we were trying to buy one house and sell another (think back to May of 2007; pretty much the exact moment the housing market crashed – and possibly the worst time in U.S. history to sell a house). Then, without notice, my sole office assistant quit. (She actually quit on a post-it note, which reminds me of a *Sex and the City* episode where Carrie's boyfriend breaks up with her on a post-it note.) My car died that month, as well. Change was happening and it was happening on steroids. *Kumbaya*!

There were many other stories from members of the women's group, some involving large sums of money arriving in the mail unexpectedly, some involving new jobs, new employees and new lovers and pets.

Law of attraction and opportunity. It's easy to explain how we attract people who vibrate similarly to us. Imagine you are at a party where you don't know anyone. You look around the room and innately select the person or people you are going to talk to. It may be what they look like that attracts you, but it is also about how their energy resonates with yours.

It is more difficult to explain how we attract opportunities and elements that vibrate similarly to us. That is where the Law of Attraction takes on more spiritual, sometimes downright magical, qualities.

Unhappy with her job, a patient of mine was complaining about her stressful situation. Instead of wallowing with her and supporting her frustration, I asked her questions about her dream job. She spoke about her ideal job with passion, detailing where it would be, what her duties would be, and what she would feel like vibrating at such a high level in her work! At the end of the visit, she was excited about her next steps. The next day, out of the blue, she was solicited by someone at her dream job. She hadn't taken any of the next steps, nor did she know that there was a job available there! This is not coincidence. It is the Law of Attraction.

A colleague of mine set up a screening booth at a popular gym. He spent an entire Saturday doing posture assessments and talking to people about chiropractic and how he could help them with their health. The next week, he got a record number of calls from new patients. None of them were people he had met at the gym the Saturday before. It was the energy he created with his actions on Saturday that set up that point of attraction for new patients to call.

Not that simple. The Law of Attraction encourages us all to live lives with purpose, vision and joy. We all have the ability to change our lives by thoughtfully refocusing our intentions. We can learn to reframe the words we use and choose what and how we think about something or someone. But as lovely as the Law is, life is not that simple. We also need to take action, to remember others with humanity and compassion, and to accept that in life there exists the positive and the negative.

Using the Law of Attraction does not mean that all you have to do is think the thought, feel the feeling, and 'poof' – your desire manifests. Sometimes the lessons learned when something doesn't manifest or go your way brings more value to your life than having the thing or reaching the goal. Carolyn Myss, in her lecture, *Energy Anatomy*, says that our version of justice is not necessarily the same as The Divine's justice. I try to find lessons everywhere, even in the hard things in life. As much as I don't like to feel uncomfortable, or sad, or depressed, that space is often where I find blessings.

The Law of Attraction has the potential to backfire. If you interpret the law too strictly, you might not let yourself feel negative emotions out of fear of attracting negative things into your life. The bottom line is, you are allowed to feel sad, or bad, or mad without worrying that a swarm of killer bees will come and attack you.

However, using the Law of Attraction mindfully can help you become more aware of your emotions and more thoughtful about the vibration you are emitting into the world. You can use that awareness to parse out where your bad feelings are coming from, see if you can derive some meaning from them, and try not to let them define you or dictate your actions.

The Buddha says that life is suffering. That does not mean life is *only* suffering, but that life is subject to impermanence – remember the concept that "change is constant"? It is the changes in life that often lead to our suffering. So how do we reconcile this basic tenet of Buddhism, which makes so much sense, with the Law of Attraction, which says that negative energy attracts more of the same? It's possible, if you are very lucky, to maintain that there does not have to be suffering in life. It is easier to say that life is directed by how positive or negative your thoughts are. It was easy in my 40's to see the Law of Attraction as the whole story. But as I have gotten older, I have seen more "stuff" happen. I've had more time to see people get sick, tragedies to occur, people to do bad things. There is a lot of potential for suffering in life.

So where is the positivity in that? Does the Law of Attraction imply that I am attracting my own suffering by talking about suffering? I wish to look at life honestly, with all of it's ups and downs. I strive every day to integrate the two poles into a worldview that is inclusive of both the positive and the negative. For that is really what life is, the yin and yang, both sides now. It's not that simple and it's not that complicated. It is everything.

Law of Attraction and Health. I am a chiropractor. I know first-hand what chiropractic adjustments do for our health. A good adjustment allows the body to function better and have a greater sense of well-being, on many levels. I did not read this in a book. I see this in my office – my patients respond to regular adjustments with increased vitality, which makes them happier, more positive people. That is why I do what I do.

I also know first hand how important lifestyle is for our health. There are ten essential lifestyle habits for healing. Along with clearing the energy (with adjustments), they include exercise, clean water, nutritious food, good sleep, good love, forgiveness, peaceful moments and gratitude, laughter, and detoxification. The Law of Attraction is a big part of why these are all important. Cleaning things out, calming things down, feeling strong and loved – these all are attributes of creating a healthy energy and vibration for the universe to bring good things our way. Yes.

However, our whole health is not dictated by the thoughts we think trickling into our emotional vibration. If that were true, we would have far less mortality from illnesses like cancer, heart disease, degenerative brain disorders and autoimmune diseases than we do. It has always felt irresponsible to give people the idea that they have total control of their health status. I know enough people who live very healthy lifestyles: Vegan, yoga-practicing people, regular chiropractic patients, in good relationships, who have done a lifetime of talk therapy who have gotten terminal cancer.

As a practitioner, I have seen many people who looked healthy and felt happy that were diagnosed with sinister things out of the blue. Obviously, if a person gets cancer or diabetes or heart disease, there is something in their body that is not working right. But there are many reasons that can happen – some are under our control and others are not. There is a blockage somewhere, it could be a bad gene or a toxicity, as well as a lifestyle problem or a stuck emotional pattern. We cannot say that they are "diseased" people, that it is their fault that they are sick. We cannot say that there is one particular issue they are not dealing with in their life, some negative vibration they have brought upon themselves that has created their situation. Just like we cannot say that it is a spinal misalignment that has brought on the situation. If that were true, chiropractors (or anyone who gets adjusted regularly) would never get cancer. Or any other disease, for that matter.

On the other hand, the Law of Attraction can affect us at the most profound level of healing. A patient of mine had suffered with a chronic pain condition for many years. When she first started coming to my office, each visit was a laundry list of issues, symptoms, descriptions of her great pain. After a few weeks of getting to know her, I suggested that for homework she make a gratitude list. A gratitude list is a simple list of things in your life for which you are grateful. When you are riddled with chronic pain, this is not an easy thing to do, so I gave her the task of just writing one thing on the list each day. I explained that even if it is "the sky is blue," it can still go on the list. The gratitude list works because of the Law of Attraction. Even focusing on a positive thing for a minute can elevate your vibration.

This exercise turned out to be life-changing for her, as she started focusing each day on the positives in her life. She still was in a good deal of pain, but she was learning how to not *be* her pain. It made a tremendous difference in her mood, how she related to others and how hopeful she felt about her own healing. One day, after two months of this exercise, she exclaimed that she was full of gratitude. She had run into an embarrassing situation and had soiled herself in her car while sitting in a parking lot. But her perspective had changed so dramatically in the months we had been working together that she saw the incident as "lucky." She felt lucky that she had not been driving. She felt lucky that she had a plastic bag within reach and it was an easy clean-up. And she felt lucky that no one saw what had happened. "Lucky" here is all about perspective. She knew that her new habit of gratitude was a major positive paradigm shift.

Vibration. The Law of Attraction is about vibration. The law says if I am vibrating in a place of judgment, fear or hatred, I am not going to feel good. I might make decisions that also don't make me feel good, or take actions that make me feel bad. If I am vibrating in a place of compassion and love, I will feel better. I will attract things to me that are vibrating equivalently.

But in the real world, just because I think positively and am loving and compassionate, I won't necessarily get only good things in my life. Jon Kabat Zinn coined the term, "Full Catastrophe Living," in his book of the same name. Full catastrophe living includes the ups and downs of life and everything in between. Using the Law of Attraction doesn't mean that I will only experience beautiful things in my life, but utilizing the Law of Attraction will help me be more successful at riding the fluctuations of life.

Practice using the Law of Attraction in your Elevate process. Practice using Law of Attraction in your daily life. Use it with good sense and compassion for yourself and others. Use it to spread love and kindness as far as you can reach.

I pay close attention to my vibration. I try to be intentional with the thoughts I think and I try my best to live with integrity. When I feel my vibration sink, I work to identify what brought on the shift and then I try to understand it. Recently, after a full day of seeing people in my office, I got an email from a long-time patient explaining that she had switched to another chiropractor. She wrote, "Thanks for your years of service and good luck!" It was a short and sweet email but in an instant, despite having a banner day doing my best work and seeing all of the wonderful people whom I am privileged to serve, I felt awful. When I got in my car, I took a few breaths and said to myself, "Nina, where is this yucky feeling coming from?" I realized that I felt rejected. It was a blow to my ego to have someone choose another chiropractor over me, and I was responding like a child. By identifying the source of the feeling and taking the two minutes to breathe and meditate, I was able to both understand her choice (she chose another excellent chiropractor), and forgive myself for reacting this way. I was eventually able to let go of that bad feeling.

And life doesn't always make sense; it's just not that simple. I pay attention to the Law of Attraction, to my vibration. I eat well, I get chiropractic, acupuncture and energy work regularly and I exercise. I have many blessings in my life. I try to be mindful of those blessings and am full of gratitude. Yet, in 2015 one of my best friends died of cancer. I had to ride that enormous wave and still hold my vibration steady for others. To make things more confusing, she was a happy, fit, productive, kind, funny, loving, mostly-vegetarian with an incredibly positive attitude about life. Life is just not simple. And it's not always easy. The yin and the yang. Both sides now.

The "Life is Good" company was founded by two brothers from the Boston area. In an interview on a local radio station, they were asked how they came up with the idea for their company. They explained that when they were boys, every night at dinner their mother had them take turns to say one good thing that happened to them that day. Obviously, their mom was tuned in to the Law of Attraction and enforced it in their home. Happily, she passed the idea on to her kids, who went on to create a wonderful company, whose motto is: "Life is not perfect. Life is not easy. But Life is Good." Exactly.

RIDING THE WAVES

The Universe works in waves. Currently we only understand a small fraction of what this encompasses. However, we can be sure that quantum physics, energy medicine, and the Universal Laws are the way of the future. And as humans who dwell in this universe, we also work in waves. We are wavy gravy.

Think about inspiration. We suddenly find the motivation to join a gym. We start journaling. We vow to do Tai Chi every day. We eat kale. For a little while we do it, and then, at some point, we stop doing it. My patients will diligently do the exercises I have recommended for a few weeks, and then they stop. They can't explain it, and they don't know why, but they stop. They know it isn't a good idea to stop, but it just happens. I start taking my vitamins daily because I know they are good for me. Yet, it is hard for me to stick to it for a very long time. Then I fall out of the habit, and I stop.

Then, one day, something spurs me back to taking them. Or I see a recipe in my inbox for vegan, paleo, soy-free spaghetti squash casserole, and it inspires me to want to go back to eating healthily. Or I remind my patient that she would be in less pain if she went back to her exercises, and she does.

So what is this wave? Is it simply human nature? Is it a measure of strength of the will? How can one combat the waves and stay consistent? If I knew the answer to these questions, and if I could harness the power of The Wave and keep everyone consistent in everything, I'd be very, very famous.

Of course there are people who have more discipline than others. You know who you are. You are people who have religious customs and rituals to which you are loyally devoted. You are people who pray at a certain time every day. You are people who do yoga or meditate every day. You are people who are driven to exercise because of competition inside or outside of yourselves. I applaud you. Yet, the majority of us have trouble sticking with long-term habits. And I say to the majority of us: forgive yourself, for you are human!

Ultimately waves are due to the Universal Law of Rhythm – everything moves in seasons and cycles. We have stages of development and patterns. We see the Law of Rhythm in our economy, our calendar, our politics, and our relationships.

Our economy counts on waves. Interest rates go down, and spending goes up. Then, to counteract that trend, interest rates are put back up, and spending goes down. I got a C+ in Economics in college (science major), but I know enough to understand that money and our entire global monetary system rides waves.

Seasons and pendulums. Our calendar has rhythms. Even in California, where it is often beautiful and sunny and mild, there are rhythms to the yearly cycle. Flora and fauna know this cycle (at least they know how it is supposed to be despite humans trying their darnedest to change it).

Politics is like a pendulum. One party is in power, things start to go downhill, that party is blamed, and then the other party comes to power, and so on. (I didn't take Political Science in college, but I understand that basic tenet. I probably would have gotten a C+
in that, too.)

Relationships have waves, as well. Sometimes you feel very close to someone and talk to her every day on the phone, and then, for no apparent reason, you lose touch and let a month or two go without contact. Or a year or two. Or ten years. But then, if you love each other and want to connect, you can call her up, and it's like no time has passed. Sometimes my children want to have a conversation with me and other times they walk around the house with earbuds in their ears.

Creativity rides the waves. You can get caught up in a creative project and produce something breathtaking, and then get stuck, blocked, feeling like that spirit will never rise out of you again. It will, and it does. People who are creative for a living say it is important to exercise the creative muscle every day, even if the ideas don't happen to be flowing that day. However, there is a fine line between having the discipline to create every day and taking the pressure off being wildly creative 100% of the time. The negative feelings of that pressure can be counter to the creative process they are trying to bring forth!

Waves and self-care. Our bodies have many cycles and rhythms. There is the rhythm of the breath. There is the rhythm of digestion (a literal wave of smooth muscle that passes your food down a long tube). There is the woman's monthly cycle. (I am convinced that men have a cycle as well; it just manifests differently. MANifests, ha!)

It always helps to have someone to remind you to make the effort, or to set up something so that you get inspired again—reading a book, signing up for a 5K race, getting a chiropractic adjustment. Set up an alert on your phone to remind you to Elevate!

Sometimes we are motivated to go all-in to achieve a goal, start a diet or workout routine, or improve something else in our lives. We think, "at last I have found the key to get me going! I will never _____ again." Um, not really.

A few years ago, my husband and I did a detox cleanse along with a program for cleaner eating. The discipline came easy. The month before, we had hosted a huge party to celebrate my son's Bar Mitzvah and, for the six months prior to the event, I had been stress-eating and too busy to make time for exercise. If you've ever planned a big party, wedding, or any other big event, you know what I'm talking about. I was more tired and sluggish than I wanted to be and felt unwell. I had gained ten pounds. I didn't feel like myself. It was time to take control, and we were motivated.

Doing it together helped, of course, as we had built-in accountability and someone else to make our smoothies for us. After about six weeks, we were feeling lighter (we lost twenty-five pounds between the two of us) and more energetic. Personally, my bowels were working better than they had in ages, always a good thing (see chapter on Gratitude), my skin was clearer and softer, my eyes were seeing better, and I had more energy. My morning wake ups at 6:00am were much less traumatic. Overall, it was a slam dunk.

I started telling my patients about the program, touting its virtues and proclaiming, "Once you have experienced the great benefits of eating well and feeling well you will never go back to your old ways." I thought I had unlocked the secret of staying motivated. My husband and I continued eating this way through the summer. We even brought a blender on our vacation so we could smoothie in the morning. It was a challenge to find unsweetened almond milk and chia seeds in rural coastal Oregon, but we did it.

However, as the school year started back up and summer turned to fall, my discipline started to wane. As the holidays approached, I was back to my sluggish ways; although I had seen the Promised Land, I wasn't able to maintain the practice. Around January, I started to beat myself up emotionally. This is not a new story, is it? I just couldn't get the motivation back. I knew what I needed to do, but it wasn't happening. I looked for guidance. A wise friend reminded me of the Law of Rhythm; my season had not come back around to motivation quite yet. But it would. And it did. It always does. It's the Law.

It is okay if you start to Elevate with excitement, which I hope you will. It's also okay if it wanes and you set it aside. You can be angry and frustrated with yourself, which I hope you won't be, or you can reach for a better feeling thought and say, "Self, that is the Law of Rhythm being expressed in my life right now. It will come back when it is time." And it will.

I recognize the waves in all humans, including myself. I acknowledge that for everything there is a season and a time for every purpose under heaven. I honor the waviness in me and I honor the waviness in you. Namaste.

When you are feeling down in the dumps, or overwhelmed, or you have too many things on your to-do list, or people are angry with you, or you are angry with people, or you can't get out of your own head, try a gratitude shift. Think of five or ten things that you are grateful for. If it's only, "I am grateful that the sun came up," that's fine. Really imagine how it feels to watch the sun come up and light up the morning sky. It will start to raise your vibration.

GRATITUDE

Dream about cancer. Not long ago, I had a dream that I was in the doctor's office. She said to me gravely, "Nina, unfortunately the test shows you have breast cancer." She showed me my MRI (which oddly looked like a scone with chocolate chips all over it, a typically weird Nina-dream image) and I immediately understood that my life was going to be shorter than I had hoped. In my dream, I started making lists of things I wanted to do with the rest of my time. In my dream, I had an argument with my husband where I yelled, "We have to figure out what's important NOW! We can't get bogged down with the stupid stuff." When I woke up, I was totally moved. Besides the scone imagery, the dream was a serious one. I knew it was neither a psychic experience nor a warning of an impending illness. Rather, it was a reminder to be more mindful of what I have in my life. I needed more gratitude.

I have walked with several friends on their cancer journey, and I don't know what that sentence feels like when it's coming down on you. I only can imagine that the sentence, "You have cancer" (after it shakes you to your core) can get your priorities in line. I have heard from many people that a terminal diagnosis can cause a shift in awareness from the mundane grumblings of life toward miracles, and can bring about more gratitude for the many tiny-nesses of life that, upon closer examination, turn out to be miracles. For instance, things like waking up and feeling the sunshine and breathing. There is no gratitude like the gratitude I felt when I woke up and realized it was a dream.

Using gratitude to help us live our best lives. "The cure for overwhelm is gratitude," one of my teachers used to say. His directive to me was, if I feel like the walls are caving in, I should reach for a "gratitude journal," write numbers 1-100 on a page, and then fill every line in with something for which I am grateful. "Right," I said. "That is really going to help solve all my problems." It seemed like a colossal waste of time. At first it was slow going. I wrote the names of my kids, my husband, my dog, my extended family, and gratitude for my work and my health. Then I was stuck. But as

I sat still and pondered over the many things I could feel grateful for, the floodgates opened. There were friends, there was nature, and color, and flowers, and animals. There was my wonderful house and my garden and my street. There was great comedy and great movies. There was Stevie Wonder. There was literature, poetry, and art. I mean, the possibilities are truly endless. I realized that I could be grateful for just breathing (and I should be!).

Observant Jews have many prayers of blessing that they say throughout the day. These prayers are usually praises of thanks to G_d for various things. My good friend, Rabbi David Jaffe, taught me that in Judaism there is a prayer that gives thanks to G_d when you go number two. It sounds far-fetched to those of us who are not used to such a thing. But really, thank goodness we have the capability to take a good poop. It cleans us out, removes toxins from our bodies, and supports our immune system. It is an important aspect of our health that we mostly take for granted, and it just feels super good. We can all add that to our gratitude list.

Grateful Vibrations. When you shift your focus onto the things for which you are grateful, you are spending time and energy thinking about things that WORK RIGHT, things that bring you joy, things that elicit positive feelings. Doing that raises your vibration.

Shifting vibration to shift emotion. As humans, we have many varying emotions. These emotions range from pure joy to utter despair, and there are an infinite number of nuanced emotions in between. The Teachings of Abraham call this the *Emotional Scale*. It is like a ladder from down-in-the-dumps all the way up to seventh-heaven.

No one can be in total joy all the time. We are humans. Our lives are variable and vulnerable to all kinds of events and changes. Sometimes we have control over our circumstances; much of the time we do not. However, we always have control over our response to our circumstances.

You don't have to make a list, you don't have to recite any specific affirmation, you don't need a recipe. Just pick something to feel grateful for, like being alive, or something or someone that makes you happy. Let yourself feel for a few moments; that is a sure way to change your vibration. Sometimes in a gratitude meditation, you may feel like your heart is so full it's going to explode. That is a wonderful way to vibrate, and it will attract other things that make your heart feel that wonderful fullness.

The Teachings of Abraham *Emotional Scale* shows that we can shift our vibration if we just concentrate on moving up the scale toward a better feeling thought than the one we are currently experiencing. In other words, if I am feeling utter despair (possibly with thoughts of hurting myself) it is unrealistic – and dangerous – to think I can shift to pure joy in a snap. But going up the scale from utter despair to anger is actually a step in the positive direction. For someone who is feeling happiness or contentment, anger does not feel like a step up. However, if you've ever felt despair, which feels hopeless and powerless, you might recognize that anger has more power inherent in it and that it is an improved feeling from despair. We don't have to go from despair to joy. We only have to take one step at a time. It will still raise our vibration and thus change our circumstances. For me, this is a most profound teaching and a simple concept. Always reach for a better feeling thought; it will change your vibration.

I use this concept in my practice all the time. I had a patient who was feeling anxious about a pain in his abdomen. It was a chronic symptom; he had been checked out multiple times in the past, and they hadn't ever found anything wrong. This time, the anxiety about the pain was getting so high that, ironically, it was making the pain much worse. Instead of suggesting he ignore it, I helped him to see that he could choose to think a different way and raise his vibration. I had him purposely think this thought, "I am so worried about this pain. What if it doesn't go away? What if I'm really sick and no one has diagnosed it yet?" I asked him how he felt, and he answered that he could feel his abdomen cramping up with worry. Then I suggested some changes to reframe the thought, a shift toward a better feeling thought. "This is the exact same pain I had before, and that was found to be nothing." "My abdomen hurts, but the pain is livable and not as bad as it was last year." "I am in good hands, and my doctor is listening to me and taking care of me." OK, these thoughts are not exactly "rainbows and unicorns" or pure joy, but they are an improvement from the first thoughts. He was able to go up the ladder a few rungs. The change in thought immediately altered his physiology, and his cramping stopped.

If you don't have the time to do the whole process, just try buzzing with a picture of gratitude. You can do it every hour on the hour or do it once a week. Either way, you will find that it works.

I use this concept with my children when they are nervous or worried about something. We try to find a better thought. "The last time you felt this way it all worked out, remember?" Finding a better feeling thought is not faking it. It's using a different truth to reframe and change your focus and thus your vibration. Upping your vibration will always help to improve your emotional state.

At the end of my Elevate meditation, I like to hang out in the Gratitude vibration for a few seconds before I open my eyes and move on with my day. All this requires is choosing an image of something that makes me instantly thankful: a loved one, being in service, or something from the natural world. Sometimes I am in total gratitude that I got my sh*t together enough to meditate that morning, and that is enough. So I vibrate with that image.

EPILOGUE

LIFTING UP

Sometimes I am in the mood for lifting up. Sometimes I have the energy to wake up early and look for the inspiring stuff, the thought-provoking stuff. Sometimes I have the bandwidth to think to myself, who can I become? How can I do better? Sometimes I am really in the mood for Elevating. And sometimes I am not. I get bogged down by life, depression, the stresses of life, the drudge, the glue I am trying to shake my hands out of, the feelings of trying to keep up with the Joneses or the Kardashians or the latest focus of want want want.

But it is exactly in these times that I do need help. And the ultimate paradox is that it is usually in these times that I am unable to seek it. I don't want it. I want to stay stuck, and that becomes my story for that moment, or for many moments (for some it is for a lifetime). And I can choose to stay stuck because it somehow feels like the place I am most comfortable. And I can choose it again and again.

Anne Lamott, in her book, *Small Victories: Spotting Improbable Moments of Grace*, opens the first chapter with these two sentences:

"The worst possible thing you can do when you're down in the dumps, tweaking, vaporous with victimized self-righteousness, or bored, is to take a walk with dying friends. They will ruin everything for you."

In the mid 2000s, I started studying Positive Psychology. I learned everything I could about how people could change their lives by shifting their thoughts into a more positive direction. I knew in my heart that a person could heal more easily and speedily if he or she could tap into this shift. Along the way, I learned from many teachers; I went to workshops and seminars, read books, listened to lectures, and talked to people. I formed a women's group that focused on shifting lives through positive attraction. It was an exciting time; I was energized and activated.

I learned, through my work and studies, that I could use these laws to attract more abundance into my life. Money had always been a tough issue for me, as growing up I had always identified as a person with not enough money, and that identity imprinted on me well into my adulthood. I began to use my knowledge to open up my life to more abundance. From the distance, it seemed an impossible task. Yet when I was ready to apply what I had learned into action, it was actually pretty simple. Like opening a window. Changing a lightbulb. Finding a new route on Waze. Going through life a slightly different way.

By my mid-forties, using the tools I had learned, I had cultivated a new outlook on money and how I identified myself around money and wealth and things that made me feel abundant. My lifestyle changed from one of lack and anxiety to one of more freedom and ease. Although the actual dollars and cents hadn't increased significantly, I felt a transformation in my soul. I felt more comfortable around money, no longer feeling like it was leaking out of my pockets. I no longer felt that at the end of the day I would have no money left.

I started allowing myself to want things: a new car, nice furnishings in my home, the newest electronics for my children. My next frontier would be attracting wealth. Why not? It is wealth that allows us to travel, to retire early, to get a house on a lake, to fund the dreams of our children, and to give to causes in which we believe. Why wouldn't I want that? It was the logical next step to freeing up my abundance mind. I made a vision board; I bought travel magazines and cut out beautiful scenes of beaches, villages

I'd like to visit, and places in Africa with beautiful smiling faces looking at the camera. I bought magazines with pictures of summer-scapes in New Hampshire, Martha's Vineyard, the Adirondacks. I spent time envisioning money flowing down a river toward me. But that next step toward wealth never felt quite right to me. Somehow, I could never get the vision to stick. It was like I didn't want it badly enough. There was a teeny war waging inside my brain between the new-abundance-me and the old-me who thought that my pursuit of wealth was materialistic, didn't really mean anything, and was selling out to the culture of want, push, get.

My mentor at the time was coaching me around this idea of wealth. His question to me always was, "What is your worthy ideal? What goal is so worth it to you that you would work your tail off, sacrifice time with your loved ones, and prioritize it above all else? What makes your heart sing?" I felt like, after all the work around abundance and money and success, it should be wealth. It should be "success" to keep striving for more. As they say in New Orleans, "mo' betta."

Then, in August of 2013, Ronna was diagnosed with Stage 4 lung cancer. Ronna was one of my closest friends in college. We met in 1983 when we were freshman. We had hardly ever gone more then a few weeks without talking since we graduated. We were old friends who knew each other in an historic way. We didn't have as much of a day-to-day friendship, where we knew what the other had had for dinner, but instead, I knew things about Ronna that no one else knew, and she knew things about me that no one else knew. It was like that.

My girlfriends from college are a close-knit group. There are eight of us; we live scattered all over the US, and we all have families and careers. On our fortieth birthdays, in 2005, we started meeting each year for a weekend of fun and frolic, loving each other up, sharing, laughing our heads off, eating great food, hiking, relaxing, and creating a signature cocktail or two. I refer to this annual event as "putting on my oxygen mask." Our girls' weekends are a place where we can all be truly ourselves, our old selves, with none of the pretensions of our current lives. Yet, at the same time, we all have respect for the women our old co-eds have become. In August of 2013, the eight of us planned a once in a lifetime girls' weekend, which included our families. There were thirty people in attendance for a summer weekend on the lake. It turned out to be a wonderful weekend, despite my initial anxiety around mixing fourteen teenagers in a house together, like Boggle cubes.

Ronna had a little cough; she explained that she was getting over a cold and still had some residual tickle. It only really showed up, she said, when she exercised. That afternoon, after swimming a mile across the lake and back, she was feeling it. We thought nothing of it and continued our festivity. And yes, Ronna swam a *mile* that day.

Two weeks later, on vacation in a small town in Italy with her family, Ronna collapsed. She was hospitalized for a week until she could get back to the States. It took another week to make the diagnosis of lung cancer.

I have lost people before. I have seen cancer take people, some slowly and steadily, others rapidly, in what seems a blink. But I had not lost someone who knew me so well, who was this much of a foundational person in my life. I had not lost someone at the peak of her life, with so much joy around her, the same age as me, who also *was* me in some ways. Defined me. Defined my sense of humor, how I think about the world, and how I don't think about the world. I'm not saying we were alike – we weren't – and we often disagreed about things. That was part of the deal with Ronna. We were history and present. We were the little things – the crossword puzzles, the Seinfeld references – and the big things – the deep, deep love and admiration, the meditation, family.

So just like that, in August of 2013 my worthy ideal was clarified and re-defined. My mirror fractured into a million pieces. Abundance defined itself differently. Life became my abundance. Years became my abundance. Time became my abundance. Mine but not hers. My family, my children, and love all took center stage in what I reached for, longed for, and desperately clung to. I did not want to work harder, strive more, give up anything. I became mindful that I actually loved my life. I loved my work, and I loved my down time. I loved spending extra time with my children. I loved my house, modest as it is, and all the things in it. I stopped trying to create, vision, and strategize around making more money, and I started paying more attention to the love I felt for my life.

I began to viscerally understand the impermanence of things. Rationally, I understood that we are all here temporarily. I had been taught it before. I had read *The Tibetan Book of Living and Dying*. But it's a whole different ballgame when it's your life that is about to have something ripped out of it. I began to understand the word "relish." I relished every moment with Ronna, every moment on the phone, every laugh, every text. I even cherished the endless voicemail messages that used to make me roll my eyes because they were so long. Because of Ronna, I began to savor every moment with anyone I cared about. I became more present, more loving and gave more smiles, hugs, and kisses. With Ronna, I couldn't sit with her without holding her hand, putting my arms around her, or leaning my head on her shoulder.

I also learned that there is an entire community of human beings that know this concept already, like anyone who has been given a life-threatening diagnosis unexpectedly, or expectedly, or like anyone who has lost a soulmate, a spouse, a loving parent prematurely, suddenly, tragically, or even naturally. This is a community that I had been lucky enough to avoid for almost fifty years. Now I was joining it.

Ronna had her own journey, which ended on this earth in September, 2015. Here is the end of the eulogy I read at her funeral:

> *"The other day I dreamed of Ronna. She was hovering over us, not as a person, but as more of a feeling. She moved her giant wings, for I have no doubt that Ronna has taken her rightful place with the angels – even though I believe it has taken her completely by surprise that they actually exist and she is like, 'No way! You guys really exist?? FUN!' In the dream, she moved her wings upward and, the way water does when you move an outstretched hand through it, the air beneath her swirled and eddied and all of us below were pulled upward with her."*

I am learning to appreciate that there are events in life that simply suck. But also that we have the ability to be lifted up by our sad times. We can learn to be enriched from tragedy. The poet Kahlil Gibran said, "The deeper that sorrow carves into your being, the more joy you can contain."

Elevate is not about being happy all the time. Elevate is a tool to help us focus, pay attention, create a little more richness in our lives. Elevate is an easy way to have a consistent practice, gain perspective, create more joy.

Life is not about being happy all the time. Life is waves, life is nuance, life is learning, life is strength. Life is not easy. Life is not perfect. But Life is Good.

READY FOR LIFT OFF

Now it is time to put it all together. Go through the process step-by-step and get ready to Elevate.

Find a quiet place and make sure there are no distractions.

Sit comfortably.

Take a few deep breaths. Look around, and see what your eyes are seeing, hear what your ears are hearing, smell your surroundings, feel your butt against the chair or the grass or the floor or your bed.

Grab your Cheat Sheet (if you need it).

Now you are ready to go.

If you are unable to do the whole process, know that it is still helpful to do part of it - pick one chakra image and one emotion and breathe!

Chakra 1: Feel the buzzing bum. Call up your image, see it in your mind, and feel the emotion it brings up. Hold this sensation for ten to twenty seconds.

Chakra 2: Feel the buzzing lower abdomen. Call up your image, see it in your mind, and feel the emotion it brings up. Hold this sensation for ten to twenty seconds.

Chakra 3: Feel the buzzing belly. Call up your image, see it in your mind, and feel the emotion it brings up. Hold this sensation for ten to twenty seconds.

Chakra 4: Feel the buzzing, expanding heart. Call up your image, see it in your mind, and feel the emotion it brings up. (Optional: See the umbrella of love reaching out to shelter those you want to offer love and compassion to or forgiveness.) Hold this sensation for ten to twenty seconds.

Chakra 5: Feel the buzzing throat. Call up your image, see it in your mind, and feel the emotion it brings up. Hold this sensation for ten to twenty seconds.

Chakra 6: Feel the buzzing third eye. Call up your image, see it in your mind, and feel the emotion it brings up. Hold this sensation for ten to twenty seconds.

Chakra 7: Feel the buzzing crown at the top of your head. Call up your image, see it in your mind, and feel the emotion it brings up. Hold this sensation for ten to twenty seconds.

When you are done, take a few seconds to feel gratitude for any number of things. Call up an image, see it in your mind and feel the emotion it brings up. Or have the Universe pour white (or golden or light purple) light down from the top of your head, and feel the goodness and gladness fill you up from the top down.

Now, go on your way, have a better day (or a peaceful sleep) and please find a way to pass it on and pay it forward.

My hope is that you make this process a part of your life each day; Elevate, breathe, buzz, and recharge.

Use this tool to reshape your day, to think a slightly different way and wake up a new flow of inspiration and happiness. Enjoy finding your own magic in Elevate. Allow it to come in, notice it fully, and – like a dog who has discovered something delicious-smelling in the grass – roll around in it with delight.

UP, UP AND AWAY.

ADDENDUM

Elevate: Nature Edition

ELEVATE WITH NATURE.

One morning, I walked out to the porch to Elevate. As I was getting my bearings, breathing in the fresh air and looking at the trees and the clouds, I felt a familiar sense of awe. "Hmm," I thought, "paying attention to nature and breathing deeply has upped my vibration. Could that be a meditation of its own?" And so it is.

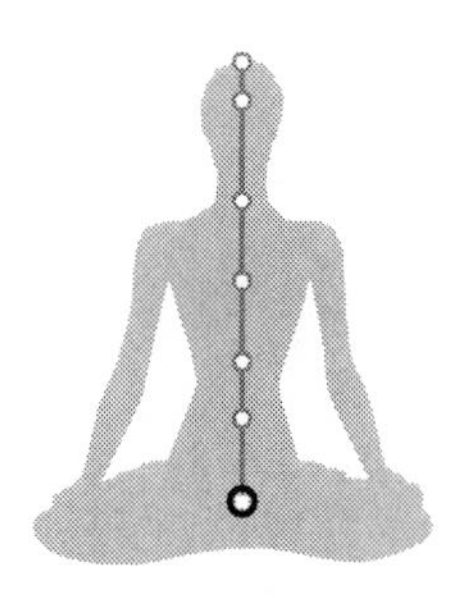

Chakra 1.

Feel the buzz in the root chakra. Visualize your self as a tall tree with roots that flow down from your first chakra deep into the earth. Feel the roots as an anchor. Feel the stability, the peace and groundedness that come from the earth, traveling up your roots, to feed you.

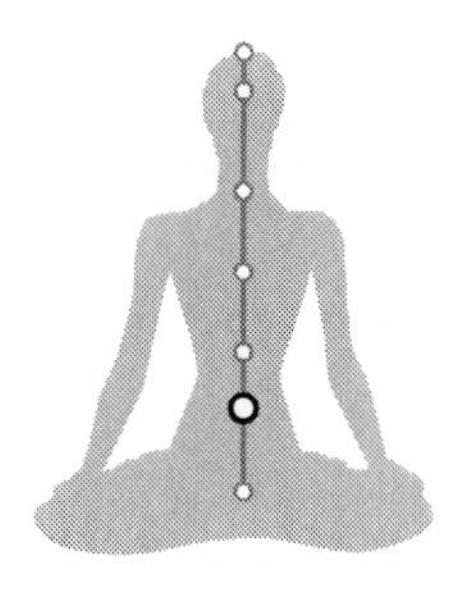

Chakra 2.

Feel the buzzing lower abdomen. Visualize a large beautiful flower blooming near your belly button. Notice the vibrant colors, the intricate shapes. I picture a tulip that comes up in my garden every year. It is huge and rose-colored with a blast of yellow and black on the inside. It is a miracle; it started as a simple bulb and yet every year it blooms into a masterful creation.

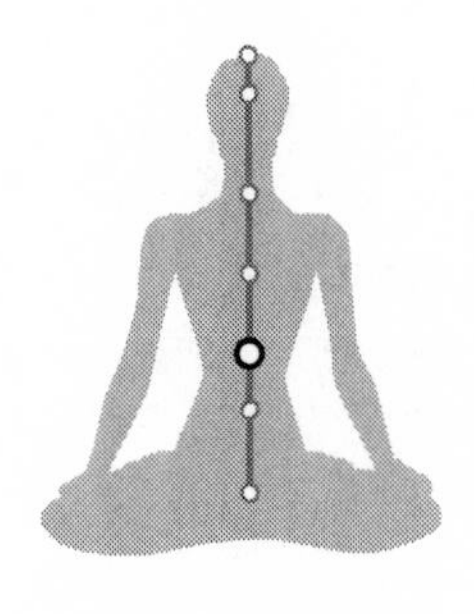

Chakra 3.

Feel the buzz in your solar plexus (belly). Imagine a majestic mountain towering before you. I think of Mount Hood, outside Portland, Oregon, with its awesome snow covered peak. The picture in my mind is from Trillium Lake, where you can see Mt. Hood's perfect reflection in the water. It is a powerful picture. The mountain is strong, unmovable, proud and confident.

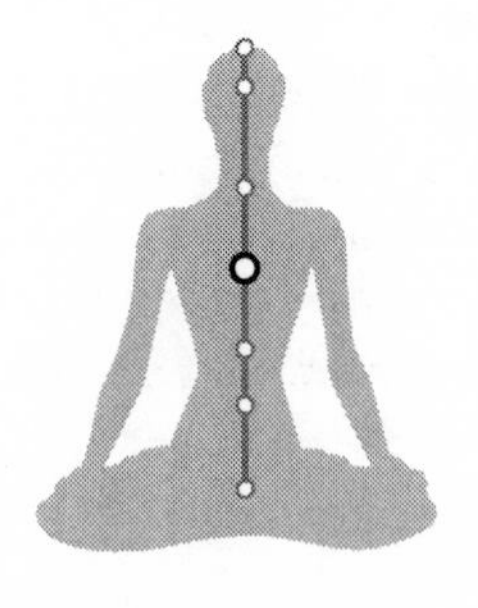

Chakra 4.

Feel the buzz in your chest and heart. Picture an animal whose eyes are loving and kind. It can be an animal with whom you have a live-in relationship (of course I think of Nellie the dog), or an animal you have not yet come to know. A baby seal? An owlet? A peaceful deer grazing in the grass? Feel the unconditional love that comes from an animal.

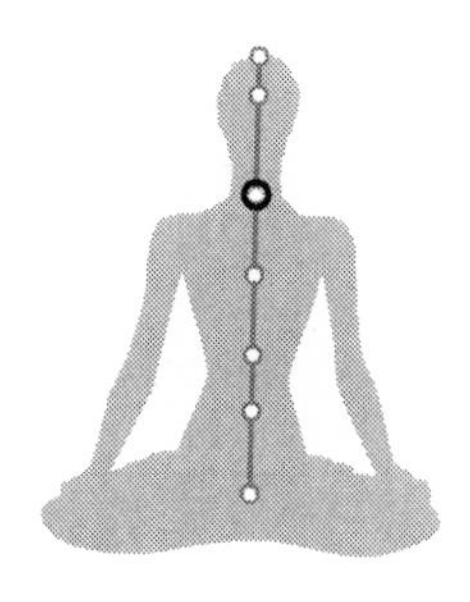

Chakra 5.

Feel the buzz in the throat. Imagine being on the ocean shore and watching the waves roll in, one by one by one. Notice the constant rhythm, dependable, eternal. Imagine you can hear the waves, the sound of them crashing over and over.

Chakra 6.

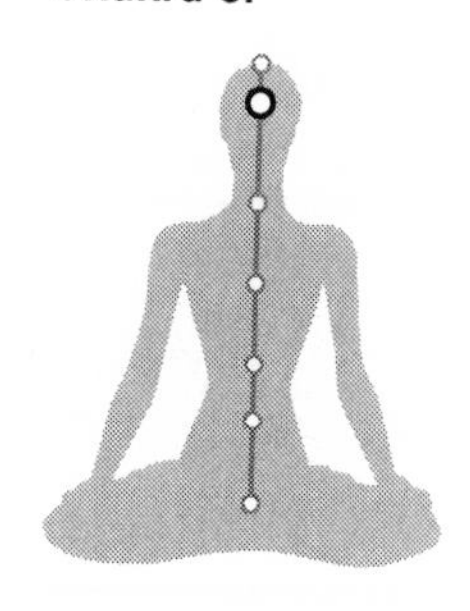

Feel the buzz between the eyebrows at the third eye. Visualize your self standing on a bridge in a forest over a river. See (and hear) the water rushing toward you, under you, away from you. Notice how you feel watching the water flow. Imagine the wisdom of the river. It always knows which way to go. It is continuous. It is sure.

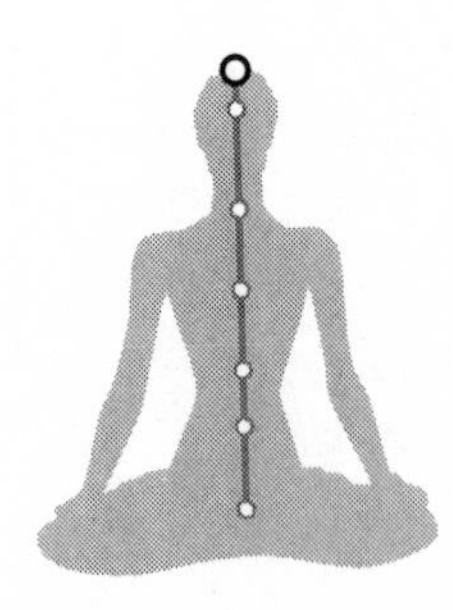

Chakra 7.
Feel the buzzing crown of your head. Imagine a dramatic sunrise or sunset with bursting beams of light streaming down from the sky and bathing you from head to toe. Feel nurtured by the light, which fills you up and makes you whole.

Gratitude: End Elevate with gratitude for the earth and its gloriousness. Feel the love and respect for all of nature.

Acknowledgments and Gratitude: I'd like to thank everyone who has supported me through this project; my family (Hi Mom!), my amazing patients, and my wonderful staff. Gratitude to my coach, Dr. Jeff Cartright, who insisted that Elevate needed to come to life, NOW. Thanks to my wonderful beta-readers; Ann, Katie, John and my sister/cousin G, who read, edited and helped me weave the fabric of words together. Gratitude to my brilliant designer, Samantha Wilder Oliver, whose eyes see things mine never could. Thank you to Nellie, with whom I walked many miles of trails while recording thoughts for this book on my phone. I am grateful to all of my oxygen masks from Tufts (BBCDKNRS 4ever) to MJ in NOLA, from Portland to Acton, all the Hosers and the Vault. Thanks to my miracles - Tessa and Abe - for believing in me with love and laughter. Most of all, great gratitude to my husband, John, who inspires and elevates me every day with his remarkable creativity and love.

Made in the USA
Middletown, DE
24 November 2017